How to
SELF-PUBLISH
YOUR BOOK
Using
MICROSOFT WORD
2010

OTHER BOOKS BY EDWIN SCROGGINS

(See them all on www.amazon.com)

BIBLE PROPHECY IN A NUTSHELL
A Mini-Survey of God's Great Plan of the Ages

STRAWBERRY LANE
A Mystical Memoir of Boyhood in Rural South Texas

RETURN TO STRAWBERRY LANE
A Mystical Memoir of Boyhood in Rural South Texas

HOW TO SELF-PUBLISH YOUR BOOK
USING MICROSOFT WORD 2007
A Step-by-Step Guide for Designing & Formatting
Your Book's Manuscript & Cover to PDF & POD
Press Specifications, Including those of CreateSpace

HOW TO SELF-PUBLISH YOUR BOOK
USING MICROSOFT WORD 2013
A Step-by-Step Guide for Designing & Formatting
Your Book's Manuscript & Cover to PDF & POD
Press Specifications, Including those of CreateSpace

HOW I BUILT MY RETREAT CABIN IN THE WOODS
AND LIVED TO WRITE ABOUT IT
A Multi-Message Memoir with Tips and Techniques
For the Do-It-Yourself Builder

THE PROMISE AND PASSION OF CHRIST THE KING
Devotional Snapshots of God's Great Plan of the Ages

SONGS IN THE NIGHT
Memories of Alma Grace Scroggins

How to
SELF-PUBLISH
YOUR BOOK
Using
MICROSOFT WORD
2010

A Step-by-Step Guide
for Designing & Formatting
Your Book's Manuscript & Cover
to PDF & POD Press Specifications,
Including Those of
CreateSpace

Edwin Scroggins

Strawberry Lane Books
Richardson, Texas

To Gene,
my late twin brother,
who worked at every task he undertook
to achieve a degree of perfection
few men could match

CONTENTS

Chapter Six   59
INSERTING PAGE NUMBERS

Chapter Eleven   119
CHOOSING YOUR PUBLISHER & SUBMITTING YOUR PDF FILES

Chapter Twelve   131
NURTURING YOUR BOOK ON AMAZON.COM

INTRODUCTION

Welcome to the latest version (as of 2010) of my book on self-publishing. This book has basically the same text as the earlier book (*How to Self-Publish Your Book Using Microsoft Word 2007*), except that I have revised the formatting procedures as required for use with Microsoft Word 2010.

If you are familiar with the use of Word 2007, but you have not yet installed and/or used Word 2010, be assured that the differences between the two versions are minimal and easily learned. Perhaps the most noticeable change is the replacement of Word 2007's "Office Button" icon (upper, left of screen) with the word "File" atop a blue background. Clicking Word 2010's **File** brings down a list of options to access that is somewhat similar to that formerly offered by the "Office Button."

When you click **File,** its menu comes up on the "Info" screen. If the document you have opened was created by any version earlier that Word 2010, one of the several choices you are given on this Info screen is to **Convert** that document into Word 2010 with its new formatting procedures. (More about this in chapter one.)

Clicking **New** on the Info menu brings up a screen on which you are given choices of a **Blank document** (for beginning a new work) and numerous **templates** for various purposes. I believe you'll find these templates interesting and possibly useful.

A few changes in tab names and other navigational terminology offer no increased difficulty of use, once you learn their functions. I figured it all out without the help of instructional books and manuals. As young as you are (I'm 83 years old at this writing), you should have no problem following my instructions.

This new book on using Word 2010 is still universally applicable for publishing with your choice of POD printers and with virtually all self-publishing firms that offer a do-it-all-yourself publishing option.

I want to emphasize here that no matter which firm you choose for self-publishing, you need use only Microsoft Word to format your book; you don't have to buy other expensive software programs. Only if you have photos or artwork inside your book or on your cover will you need access to an inexpensive program like Adobe Photoshop Elements: *Elements,* not the full Photoshop program. If your book's text and cover have no photos or artwork, you will need only Microsoft Word to format them.

And now, a few disclaimers: First, this book is *not* a manual on how to write *your* book. You should look elsewhere for help with writing if you need it. Next, this book will *not* teach you to operate a computer, and it will *not* explain the *basics* of using a word processor. And finally, you will *not* learn how to promote and market your book. I am leaving these lessons to other teachers and writers.

Assuming you already have *basic* computer and word processing skills (but you *don't* have experience in book design or in conversion of a manuscript to PDF), this book *will* lead you step-by-step through all the decisions, designs, and formatting procedures you must negotiate in order to get your book into print.

Perhaps you are reading this Introduction in order to decide whether or not you want to buy this book. Why, you are asking, should I buy this book when there are so many others like it, some of which have been written by successful authors with recognizable names?

I admit that my competing with these authoritative authors seems foolish, but my book offers what none of their books provide. Their books do, in fact, contain valuable knowledge on each phase of the self-publishing process. But none of them I have read thus far carries its instructions for *all* the required design and formatting procedures down to the final *step-by-step* level. In many instances, you have to work out the details of their instructions for yourself. But if you will follow *my* instructions to the letter, you won't be stymied at any point in the publishing procedure, and you *can* and *will* get your book published.

Some of you who begin reading this book may become regretful about having bought it when you discover that its early chapters deal with commands and procedures you already know. I have included these chapters in order to cover *all* the potential problems that even a few readers might face. I hasten to advise you that later chapters get progressively more complex, and that they offer instructions for tasks that you may never have performed.

One final word: I do believe that my instructions on the features addressed by this guide will be worth the paltry sum you must pay or have already paid for it. But, if it doesn't work for you the way I intend it to, I cannot be responsible for any financial losses that result from its use, nor can I be held accountable for the stress, nervous breakdown, or other forms of mental anguish the guide's failure might cause you to experience.

I am tempted to say "good luck," but you won't need luck if you follow my instructions carefully.

How to
SELF-PUBLISH
YOUR BOOK
Using
MICROSOFT WORD
2010

Chapter One

FORMATTING YOUR PAGES
WITH MICROSOFT WORD

To facilitate your recognition of what is required of you when confronted by a series of computer commands and chains of dialog boxes, I have, throughout this book, presented my instructions in the following form:

All commands that you must **click** and all options you must **select** are set in **bold** letters or numbers.

All Dialog boxes requiring action on your part are labeled with UPPER CASE letters.

PRELIMINARY ADVICE

There are three ways to design a book: (1) You can reformat a new, blank Word document and then compose your text on it, (2) You can reformat a new, blank Word document and then insert your already completed Word manuscript into it, or (3) You can bring up your already completed Word manuscript and then change its page setup and other formatting to make your book look like you want it to look when your POD printer prints it.

If you intend to use method (3) to reformat a manuscript created by a Word version earlier than Word 2010, you can elect to **Convert** that document to Word 2010. When you open your manuscript, click **File** at the top, left of your screen. The menu will open on "Info" and show that your manuscript file is in "Compatibility Mode." If you want to convert your file to Word 2010, click **Convert** on the INFO dialog box. To see the advantages and disadvantages of converting your file, see the notes to the right of the "Convert" box. Leaving your file in "Compatibility Mode" will not affect this book's instructions.

Whether you are going to reformat a new, blank Word document or your already completed manuscript, I strongly advise that you make and use templates in the process. Assuming you are beginning with a new, blank Word document, you first set up your page size, page margins, page layout, line spacing, and font choices as instructed below. Then click **Save** and navigate to the location in which you want the file saved. Name the file "1. Page Setup" and click **Save** again. You will now have a template of your new page setup to use for whatever you write or insert manuscripts into. I have preceded the title of this template, and each template to follow, by a number that represents the order in which it should appear in your menu of templates.

If you start with your already completed manuscript and plan to change its formatting to match your book requirements, be sure to do a **Save As** on the original manuscript so that you will still have available your original, unmodified copy. Then follow the same template-making steps mentioned above and below as you work on it.

The first time you save your work on any template, always use **Save As** so that the original template will remain unaltered and available for other uses or for starting fresh again if you mess up what you have been using it for.

After you use your "1. Page Setup" template to write on or to insert your manuscript into, make another renamed template of that template, using **Save As** before beginning to insert section breaks. (I'll explain what section breaks are later on.) Then make another template of that template after inserting section breaks but before inserting page numbers. If you mess up any of this and want to start over, you can delete your mess and bring up a new copy of your manuscript on your previously designed page layout, or you can retrieve another template with section breaks already inserted.

Anyway, I'll now move on to showing you how to format your book's pages. This chapter will provide all of the instructions you need to format your book's pages to meet the specifications of whatever self-publishing firm you choose. I'll begin by showing you how to format a new, blank Word document.

FORMATTING YOUR PAGES WITH WORD 2010

If you haven't already done so, activate the "ruler" on your screen. Click the **View** tab and then select **Ruler** in the "Show" group. You won't have to do this every time you turn on your computer. The Ruler will remain on your screen. This will be especially useful when you begin formatting your book's cover in chapter nine.

One other thing you need to activate is the **Show/Hide** symbol. To do this, click the **Home** tab and in the "Paragraph" group, click the little **icon** that looks like the letter "P" turned backwards. This symbol will now appear at the beginning of all blank lines and at the end of each line of text when you press **Enter** on your keyboard.

Setting Page Trim Size, Margins, & Layout
When formatting a new, blank Word document, the very first thing you should do is to decide what size you want your book to be: 5.25" x 8", 6"x 9," etc. (The book's width is always specified first.) Both the front and back covers of your book and its interior pages will all be cut to this "trim" size. And, the trim size you choose must match one of the sizes specified as acceptable by your POD printer. Most self-publishing firms offer a variety of trim sizes they will accept. I prefer 6" x 9," but you may want another size.

Setting Your Page Trim Size
Bring up a new, blank Word document in Print Layout view. (To access the Print Layout view, click the left **icon** at the bottom, right of your screen.) Set up your page trim size as follows: Click the **Page Layout** tab on the top menu bar. In the "Page Setup" group, click the little **arrow** at the bottom, right corner of the box. On the PAGE SETUP dialog box that comes up, click the **Paper** tab and enter the following:

Paper tab:

Paper size:	Choose your own page size below.
Width: **6"**	Enter width & height or use arrows.
Height: **9"**	

Apply to:	**Whole document** Click **arrow** to select.
	OK Don't click this. Click the **Margins** tab on the PAGE SETUP dialog box.

Setting Your Margins
Margins tab   Choose your own dimensions below.
   Margins
      Top: **1"**   Bottom: **1"**
      Left: **0.75"**   Right: **0.75"**
      ("Left" changes to "Inside" and "Right" changes to
      "Outside" when you check "Mirror margins" below.)
      Gutter: **0**   Leave this default.

   Orientation
   Portrait   Select this.

   Pages
      Multiple pages: **Mirror margins**   Click arrow to
                                              select.

      Apply to: **Whole document**   Click arrow to select.
                  OK   Don't click this. Click the **Layout** tab
                            on the PAGE SETUP dialog box.

Choosing Your Layout Options
Layout tab
   Section
      Section start: **Odd page**   Click arrow to select.

   Headers and footers
      Different odd and even   Check this box.
      Different first page   Check this box.

      From edge: Header: **0.4"**   Enter this.
                   Footer: **0.4"**   Enter this.

Page
    Vertical alignment: **Top**   Leave this.

    Apply to: **Whole document**   Click arrow to select.

                OK   Now click this.

Setting Line Spacing

When submitting a manuscript to a conventional publisher, you are almost always required to double-space lines. However, for a print-on-demand book, your manuscript must appear just as you expect it to look when printed. You could just stick with Word's default "1.15" line spacing, but your text will be easier on the reader's eyes if you space your lines slightly more apart than Word's default spacing provides.

    "Experts" on line spacing say that lines should be spaced 2 to 4 points more than the font size you are using. Text printed in 12-point font size, for example, should have its lines spaced 14 to 16 points apart. (The lines you are reading are in 12-point and are spaced 16 points apart.)

    To change Word's default line spacing, click the **Home** tab on the top menu bar**.** In the "Paragraph" group, click the **Line and Paragraph Spacing icon** and then click **Line Spacing Options** on the options list that comes up. On the PARAGRAPH dialog box that comes up, enter the following:

    Indents and Spacing tab
        Spacing
           Line spacing:
           Exactly   Click arrow to select.

(handwritten margin note: Use Format → Paragraph)

Now click the **arrow** on the "At" options window and enter your font point number + **2** or + **3** or + **4.** (If you are using **12** point font and you add **4** points, the number in the window will now be **16 pt**.)

Now under "Spacing," click the **arrows** to show **0 pt** in both the "Before" and "After" windows.

Then click **OK**. Your line spacing is now set for the entire document.

If you want your selected line spacing to become Word's "Default" spacing for all Word documents that you write, do the following:

In the "Paragraph" group, click the **Line and Paragraph Spacing icon** again, and then click **Line Spacing Options** on the options list that comes up. On the PARAGRAPH dialog box that comes up, under the "Indents and Spacing" tab, click **Set As Default** at the bottom of the box. On the MICROSOFT WORD dialog box that comes up, select "All documents based on the Normal template?" Then click **OK**. Your line spacing is now set for all Word documents in the "Normal" template.

However, if you are spacing your lines at anything above *single space*, re-spacing *some lines* back to single space is sometimes necessary before inserting photos or other images. You may have great difficulty with such insertions if you do not, beforehand, go to the page on which you intend to insert your photo, click your cursor on the **line** at which you want the **top** of your photo to appear, and change *only* that line to **single** space. (More about image insertion in a later chapter.)

No doubt you already know how to "justify" your lines. I mention this here in order to remind you that you will have to re-justify those text blocks you later compose, insert, or copy and paste into your formatted pages.

Choosing Fonts & Font Sizes
There is much to learn about fonts (typefaces), but I will mention only a few necessary things to consider:

Serif Fonts
Serif fonts are those that have little curlicues and projections at the ends of their main strokes:

> This is a serif font, lower case, Georgia, 12 point.
> THIS IS A SERIF FONT, UPPER CASE, GEORGIA,
> 12 POINT.

These embellishments are used, supposedly, for decoration and for making the text easier to read. You should use "TrueType" serif fonts for the interior text of your book. (Some authors prefer to use sans serif fonts—described below—for interior headings, chapter titles, etc.) Many good TrueType fonts are already installed in Microsoft Word. But don't use Word's "Times New Roman." It is a somewhat condensed font, normally used for newspaper columns. The serif font I am using for this book is Georgia, 12 point. Look at other serif fonts that Word provides and choose one you like. Be sure to specify your font choice in your page setup. In Word 2010, font types and sizes can be selected under the **Home** tab's "Font" group.

Sans Serif Fonts

Sans serif fonts are simply fonts without serifs:

This is a sans serif font, lower case,
Verdana, 12 point

THIS IS A SANS SERIF FONT, UPPER CASE,
VERDANA, 12 POINT

In his book *Perfect Pages*, Aaron Shepard advises his readers to use a sans serif font such as Verdana on the front covers and spines of their books. I took his advice on the first seven books that I self-published; I used Verdana as large in font size as I could squeeze into available spaces on covers and spines. On my books' back covers, I used the serif font Georgia in various point sizes.

However, on the eighth, ninth, and tenth books I self-published, and on this eleventh book, I decided to go against Aaron's recommendation and use the serif font Georgia on my books' covers and spines as well as for their texts. You can judge for yourself as to which fonts you like best.

Font Size

As to the size of fonts you should use for text, 10 point is too small. I suggest using 12 point. Some authors use larger sizes for chapter titles, headings, etc.

For your book's front cover and spine, use fonts as large as possible. On your book's interior text, however, you may run into a problem if you use a very large font for your book's title on the title page, or for chapter titles, etc. The large font may become clipped-off by your use of greater than single space between lines. If this happens, you can reduce the large font size, or you can reformat only that *single* large font line to **single** space. This will correct the problem.

These few suggestions should be adequate for choosing the fonts for your book's text and cover. For those of you who want more details about fonts, I recommend you purchase from amazon.com Aaron Shepard's above mentioned book, *Perfect Pages*. His book also contains much other valuable information related to book design and formatting.

This concludes the formatting of your book's pages, but you can make changes any time you want by returning to the formatting menus to insert new choices. Now that you are through with this task, **save** your work as "1. Page Setup."

We will make a template from this Page Setup file when we get to chapter 3. I will tell you then what to name that template.

Chapter Two

DESIGNING YOUR BOOK BLOCK

Having formatted a single page for your book—a page format that will duplicate itself throughout the book's entire interior—you are now ready to design your "book block." This chapter will not ask you to *do* anything yet with your book; it contains only instructions on what to consider when you do actually begin to create your own book design.

If you have ever submitted a full manuscript to a potential publisher, you may already be familiar with most of the material in this chapter. Nevertheless, I believe your time will be well spent in reading it. You can compare what you already know with what you read here.

WHAT IS A BOOK BLOCK?

The term "book block" is what publishers use to denote all the pages between the covers of a book. These pages not only include the text, but also all photos, drawings, or other illustrations included in a book. Your ready-to-print book block must, obviously, include all these interior pages in the correct order, with page numbers, headers, and/or footers inserted.

GENERAL ORDER OF BOOK ELEMENTS

When people read a book, many of them pay little attention to all those "front matter" pages preceding the actual beginning of the book. They seldom are interested in the copyright page or the dedication, and few even bother to read the table of contents. But even so, a properly designed book should include at least a few basic front matter pages. And, according to a general consensus among book design style guides, these pages should appear in a certain order.

A "page," in this context, means *one side* of a two-page sheet in a book. A page can be "verso" (left, even-numbered) or "recto" (right, odd-numbered). According to *The Chicago Manual of Style*, the following book elements should *always* be placed on recto (right, odd-numbered) pages. And, these pages must be placed in the order listed below. (The copyright page is enclosed in parentheses because, in this list, it, *only*, does not appear on a recto page. It is included here to preserve the order of required pages.)

Book Elements on Recto Pages
First half title (contains only the book's main title, less subtitle)
Title page (book's title, subtitle, author's name, and publisher)
(Copyright page, always appears on *verso* page that immediately follows title page.)
Dedication
First page of Table of Contents
First page of foreword, preface, acknowledgments, introduction, prologue, or any other section included as front matter

Second half title

First part title (if any) and all consecutive part titles

First page of text (introduction, prologue, chapter 1, or whatever begins text)

First page of each chapter in *nonfiction* books. (Exception: in autobiographies and memoirs, authors often place the first page of each chapter on whatever page follows the last page of the previous chapter.) In *fiction* books, chapter first pages may also appear on verso pages.)

First page of each section in back matter

Optional Choices

Although some authors insert acknowledgments and/or other pages between the dedication and table of contents, the order of elements above and below such optional insertions should remain as listed above. I strongly advise those of my readers who are not familiar with the inclusion and placement of book elements to study the construction of a wide sample of fiction and nonfiction books.

These rules are for those of you who wish to follow the book industry's accepted style guides. Since you will be self-publishing your own book, you do not have to pattern it after these dictates. Choose your own style if you want to buck publishing conventions.

DESIGNING YOUR BOOK'S FRONT MATTER

Although the page plan below repeats, to some extent, the above list of all pages required to be placed on recto (right, odd-numbered) pages, the following includes *all* pages that make up front matter only:

Actual Page	Given Num.	Visible Num.	Book Element
1	i	-	1st Half Title
2	ii	-	Blank*
3	iii	-	Full Title
4	iv	-	Copyright Page
5	v	-	Dedication
6	vi	-	Blank**
7	vii	-	Contents-page 1
8	viii	viii	Contents-page 2
9	ix	-	Introduction-page 1***
10	x	x	Introduction-page 2

*   On actual page 2, you may insert your book's series title (if any), a frontispiece (thematic illustration), or a list of your previous publications, or you may leave the page blank.

**   On actual page 6, you may include an epigraph, acknowledgments, or other text, or you may leave it blank.

*** Instead of an "Introduction" on actual page 9, you may prefer to insert a prologue, preface, foreword, or other front matter material. For elements having more than one page, all pages of those elements beyond their first pages (including those of "Contents") should receive visible numbers. As suggested above, a study of several recently published fiction and nonfiction books may be beneficial.

DESIGNING YOUR BOOK'S TEXT LAYOUT

Authors use so many variations in designing the page layout of their books' texts that you are largely left to your own whims and preferences. A few guidelines, however, may help you navigate through some of these choices.

As stated above, in non-fiction books (excluding autobiographies and memoirs), the first page of all chapters and other text elements (including "Part" pages) must appear on recto (right, odd-numbered) pages. I will tell you how to make them do this when we get to a later chapter that deals with inserting section breaks.

Chapter titles sometimes are positioned at the very tops of their pages, but most authors and/or publishers drop such titles about a third or half way down their pages. The number of blank lines left between a chapter's title and the beginning of the text varies from one or two to a large number. Chapter titles are usually centered on their pages and are sometimes in sans serif and larger fonts. Again, I suggest you study several recently published fiction and nonfiction books for ideas. But whatever layout you choose for your own book's text, be sure to be consistent, from chapter to chapter, in applying your design.

If you will be importing/inserting your previously written manuscript into your new page layout, that manuscript will probably have been double-spaced to meet the submission requirements of various publishing houses you hoped would publish your book. This means that you will, obviously, have to reformat your text once you import it. Also, your text will not have included whatever photos and/or illustrations you intended to have your publisher insert. In a later chapter, I will include comments on inserting and positioning photos and other illustrations within your text.

DESIGNING YOUR BOOK'S BACK MATTER

Back matter consists of one or more of the following elements, not necessarily inserted in the order listed:

Acknowledgments (if not in front matter)
Appendix
Notes
Glossary
Bibliography or References
Contributors
Index
Author biography

Other elements such as Chronology, Abbreviations, and Illustration Credits may also be placed in back matter if they do not appear elsewhere.

As stated earlier, the first page of all back matter elements should be placed on recto (right, odd-numbered) pages. Should your book have more than one appendix, the first page of the second and subsequent appendices can be placed either on recto *or* verso pages.

With these requirements concerning your book's front matter, text, and back matter in mind, you are now ready to begin writing or inserting your manuscript into your "1. Page Setup" template.

Chapter Three

INSERTING YOUR MANUSCRIPT

Repeating my comments on the first page of chapter two, I suggest that there are three ways to design a book: (1) You can reformat a new, blank Word document and then compose your text on it, (2) You can reformat a new, blank Word document and then insert your already completed Word manuscript into it, or (3) You can bring up your already completed Word manuscript and then change its page setup and other formatting to make your book look like you want it to look when your POD printer prints it.

If you previously chose method (3), you probably are well on your way to formatting your book block, except for the insertion of photos, illustrations, section breaks, page numbers, and header text, all of which we'll consider in future chapters.

If you now intend to use method (1), you don't need to import a manuscript; you can just begin writing your book on a **Save As** copy of your newly made "1. Page Setup" template. Rename it "2. Book Block."

If you prefer method (2), you are now ready to begin inserting your previously written manuscript. And, again, before you begin this procedure, be sure to make a **Save As** copy of your "1. Page Setup" template and rename it "2. Book Block."

INSERTING A FILE OR MULTIPLE FILES

The first way to import your manuscript file or files into your "2. Book Block" template is that of using "Insert." To begin, click your cursor on the template at the place you want the chapter or other book element to begin. Click **Insert** on your top tool bar menu. On that menu, go to the "Text" group and click the "Object" icon's *arrow* (not the icon, itself). Then click **Text from File**.

In the INSERT FILE dialog box that comes up, locate and **double-click** the file you want or **select** it and click **Insert** at the bottom of the box. The end of your selected file will appear on your formatted page, and you will have to scroll up to find its beginning.

Now look closely at your inserted text. Depending on what the insertion's original font, font size, line spacing, and other formatting was, and what "Style" it was originally created in, its formatting *may* or *may not* match that of your book block template. If it *doesn't* match, do the following:

Click your cursor at the beginning of your insertion's **Title** or at the beginning of its **first line** if it doesn't have a title. Then scroll to the end of the insertion and, while holding down the **Shift key,** click your cursor on the right side of the very **last letter** or **character** in the insertion. Let up on the shift key after the text becomes highlighted.

Now, in the "Home" tab's "Styles" group, click your cursor on the little **arrow** at the lower, right corner of the box. At the top of the menu that drops down, click **Clear All**. All the previous formatting of the inserted text will be cleared, its "Style" will read "Normal," and its font and line spacing will revert to Word's *default* font and line spacing. If you previously changed Word's default font and line spacing, your inserted file will revert to that font and line spacing.

(These changes in Word's default font or line spacing can be made by clicking the **arrow** at the bottom, right corner of either the "Font" or "Paragraph" group under the "Home" tab. Then select your **font** or **line spacing**, click **Set As Default** at the bottom of either box, and, on the MICROSOFT WORD dialog boxes that come up, select **All documents based on the Normal template** and click **OK**.)

Close the STYLES dialog box. With the entire insertion still highlighted, change the inserted text's **font** and **font size** (if necessary) in the "Home" tab's "Font" group. In the "Paragraph" group, click **Justify** and then click the **Line and Paragraph Spacing Icon** to check or to set the inserted text's line spacing to match that of your book block template. (See page 8 in chapter one if you've forgotten how to do this.)

Now click anywhere on the page to remove highlighting. In the "Home" tab's "Paragraph" group, **Center** headings that need centering. In the "Font" group, insert **bold** or **italic** letters where necessary. Using the ruler above your text, **indent** paragraphs, quotations, and other matter as required.

If your manuscript was previously prepared for a prospective publisher (who rejected it), you probably already have divided that manuscript into numerous files, one for the front matter, one for the back matter, and one for each chapter in your text. In this case, you will have to perform this insertion procedure many times, positioning each succeeding chapter immediately following the last one inserted.

If your manuscript was all contained in one, lengthy file, you will have only one insertion to do. But when it comes to inserting files for a book, I really like being able to insert one chapter at a time. You usually have to do lots of cleanup after each insertion. I would rather correct all of this one chapter at a time than to be faced with an entire manuscript in disarray.

COPYING & PASTING A FILE OR MULTIPLE FILES

The second method of importing files is that of using **Copy** and **Paste**. To copy and paste a single-file chapter or other single-file book element into your "2. Book Block" template, click your cursor on the template at the place you want the chapter or other book element to begin. Navigate to the **file** you want to copy and **Open** it. Then **highlight** the entire file. (See above on how to do this.). Now click **Copy** on the "Home" tab's "Clipboard" menu, or, **right-click** on the highlighted file and click **Copy** on the drop-down menu. Return to your template by **closing** the file you copied. Click **Paste** on the "Home" tab's "Clipboard" menu, and the end of the chapter will magically appear. Scroll up to find its beginning.

Obviously, if the file you copy and paste has formatting that doesn't match that of your book's template, you will have to reformat that file using the procedure described above.

If your entire manuscript is in one large file, you must **Open** that file and bring up the chapter or element that you wish to copy. **Highlight** that entire chapter or element, and then **Copy** and **Paste** it into your book block. Repeat this procedure for every chapter and element in your book.

As to copying and pasting your entire manuscript all at once, try it if you like, but be warned that there will be lots of reformatting and cleanup to be done. I would rather do this one chapter at a time.

Chapter Four

PREPARING & INSERTING IMAGES

Some POD printers and self-publishing firms allow you to insert black & white photos and other images into your book block at no extra charge, but including photos inside your book presents additional problems you may wish to avoid.

Having to insert extra section breaks to isolate these photos is a relatively minor problem (more about this in the next chapter), but the real difficulty lies in getting pictures processed and printed at the *quality* you want. In publishing my own memoir books with BookSurge, I learned this the hard way. My photos turned out to look far different in the printed books than they had looked on my computer's screen. (See these photos in my *Strawberry Lane* and *Return to Strawberry Lane* memoir books listed on Amazon.com.)

In my first memoir book, *Strawberry Lane*, my pictures mostly all look much darker and more poorly defined than I expected they would look. However, in my second memoir book, *Return to Strawberry Lane*, my photos look much better. I finally learned how to process them in a way that resulted in optimum quality.

But even at their best, photos printed, at this time, by a POD press will not compare with pictures from your camera, printed by your own photo printer. And, to get even the quality a POD press *can* produce, you will have to buy, or gain access to, a minimal photo processing program such as Adobe Photoshop Elements (not the costly, full Photoshop, but the less expensive "Elements" version, about $79 or so after rebate). But, if you are still determined to include photos in your book, read on.

I'm going to give you my take on everything you need to do to prepare and insert your photos and/or other illustrations, assuming you have some to put in your book. I will present these instructions in two parts:

1. Capturing and Processing Your Images
2. Inserting Your Images

CAPTURING & PROCESSING YOUR IMAGES

Any photo or other image you upload to your POD printer or self-publishing firm should have a *minimum* resolution of 300 dpi (300 dots-per-inch or 300 ppi, pixels per inch). Since whatever device *originally* "captures" or creates an image sets that image's *original* resolution, you must use care in selecting or creating your images.

Using Photos from a Digital Camera

If you take photos for your book with a digital camera that has a 300 dpi capability (at the maximum size that you need), you're all set. You can just load the photos from your camera into your computer for processing. However, some inexpensive digital cameras that were manufactured years ago take photos at far less than 300 dpi resolution at a size that is too small to permit satisfactory "resampling." With inexpensive software like Adobe Photoshop Elements, you *can* resample low-resolution images to increase their resolution, but this may reduce their sizes (at 300 dpi) to less than desirable dimensions.

Newer digital cameras on the market today take pictures with more-than-adequate resolution. At first glance, this may not seem to be true. My own digital camera, for example, takes photos of a huge size (18.133 inches wide by 13.6 inches high) at 180 dpi resolution. Obviously, the 180 dpi resolution is not adequate, but because of the photos' large size, their resolution can be satisfactorily changed to 300 dpi. This can be done by first **deselecting** Photoshop's "Resample" function and then changing the photos' resolution to **300 dpi.** Then by **reselecting** "Resample," the photo's sizes can be specified as desired (up to a maximum size limit) without degrading photo quality.

Later on in this chapter, I will tell you exactly how to resample your digital camera's big-sized, low resolution photos to meet the 300 dpi requirement, but for now, just download them from your camera to your computer and **save** them *as they are* in "My Pictures" or in another location of your choice. You might want to create a folder to put them in. Label the folder "My book's photos, originals from camera."

Using Photos from a Film Camera
Chances are that your photos (especially for a memoir) were taken long ago with a roll-of-film camera. The resolution of these developed and printed pictures is more than adequate. Then all you need to do is to scan them with a good quality scanner, a procedure during which you can specify the

resolution at which you want the photos scanned. (Because high resolution is already there on the developed photo.)

Using Handmade Artwork & Images

Not only can you set the resolution of high-quality photos that you scan, you can also set the resolution as you scan any handmade artwork or drawings you wish to include in your book. Your scanner, of course, does not endow such images with high resolution; they already have it. You are thereby allowed to set your scanner's scan to the resolution you want. But be wary of some clipart and photos that you might download and insert. Such images are not always of adequate resolution.

To repeat myself, *original* resolution is established by the device that *originally* "captures" or creates your photos and other images. Since the device that captures an image has permanently set the total number of *original* pixels, just enlarging that image will not increase its resolution.

Scanning Photos & Artwork

I have and use a Hewlett Packard Scanjet G4050 that I bought recently. If you are using an earlier or different model HP scanner or one other than a Hewlett Packard, you will have to adapt my instructions to your own scanner.

When I bring up my scanner's "Solution Center" page, under "Start an activity" I am given four choices. One of them is "Scan Picture." When I click the **Scan Picture** option, the SCANNING FROM dialog box comes up. On it, I click **Picture to File**. On the right side of the box is a list of default scan settings. I don't like some of the settings, so I click **Change**

Settings. This brings up a number of options on the right side of the box.

I click one of these options named **Advanced Picture Settings**. On the ADVANCED PICTURE SETTINGS dialog box that comes up, among the options I am offered is a window for the selection of "Output Resolution (ppi)." The default figure in the window is set at "200." I click the window's **arrow** and select **300**.

In the same dialog box I am offered "Quality vs. Speed." I choose the **quality** option and click **OK** at the bottom of the box. This returns me to the SCANNING FROM dialog box, where I can select other scanning options.

The "Output Type" window's **arrow** allows me to choose from "Color," "GrayScale," or "Black and White." Since I am going to process my photos later in Adobe Photoshop Elements, and since the picture I am scanning is in color, I choose **Color.**

For the "File Type" window, I click its **arrow** and select **RGB**. (I will convert the picture later to Grayscale in Photoshop.)

When I finally click **Scan** at the bottom of the box, the SAVE TO FILE SAVE OPTIONS dialog box comes up and asks me to name my file and to accept the default save location or to specify the location in which I want my picture saved. I name my file, accept the default save location, and click **OK** at the bottom of the box.

After a pause, the "HP Scanning" screen comes up, and the scanner finally scans the picture. But this is not the final scan. This scan is for the purpose of altering the picture in numerous ways, including "Rotate/Flip," "Crop," "Resize

Output," "Lighten/Darken," "Adjust Color," and "Correct Picture."

I don't want to do any adjustments or corrections now, so I click **Finish** at the bottom of the screen to initiate the final scan. My scanner scans the picture as it is and sends it to the save location I specified.

Since my new scanner has picture processing capabilities similar to those of Adobe Photoshop Elements, I *could* process my pictures while scanning them without using Photoshop Elements or any other picture processing software. But some scanners have more limited capabilities, so I will leave my photo unprocessed by my scanner and import that picture into Photoshop Elements for final processing.

Processing Images with Photoshop Elements

The photos you have saved from your digital camera are most likely in *RGB* color mode, of *less* than *300 dpi* resolution, and probably in *JPEG* format. Photos from most scanners are in *Indexed Color* or *RGB Color* mode, of *300 dpi* resolution that you set while scanning, and in *Bitmap* or *JPEG* format. Most self-publishing firms using POD presses require that all black-and-white images in your book's *interior* be submitted in *Grayscale* mode, *300 dpi* resolution, and *JPEG* format.

To make these conversions—along with editing your pictures—I suggest the following procedures. I use Photoshop Elements, version 9.0. If you use an earlier version, or any version later than 9.0, adapt my instructions to your own version.

Processing Digital Cameras' Images for Interior Pages
First, for photos you will use inside your book, we will change your digital camera's photos to 300 dpi resolution:

1. Bring up Photoshop Elements.
2. Click the **Edit** button, not the "Organize" button.
3. On the screen that comes up, click **File** on the top menu bar. On the drop-down menu, click **Open**.
4. Navigate to the picture you want to process, select the picture, and click **Open** at the bottom of the screen.
5. On the menu bar at the top of the page, click **Image**. On the drop-down menu that appears, position your cursor over "Resize" and click **Image Size.** On the IMAGE SIZE dialog box that comes up, you will see under "Document Size" the Width, Height, and Resolution of the photo. At the bottom of the IMAGE SIZE dialog box, **deselect** (click **off** the check in) the "Resample Image" box. Now type **300** into the "Resolution" box above. This changes the "Width" and "Height" dimensions into the maximum size your photo can be at 300 dpi resolution. But don't click "OK" yet.

Next, we will resize your digital camera's photo to the size you want it to appear inside your book:

6. Now that the photo is at 300 dpi, you can make it smaller without degrading its quality. To do this, put a **check** in both the "Resample Image" box and the "Constrain Proportions" box at the bottom of the IMAGE SIZE dialog box. Now enter the smaller dimension you want into either the "Width" box or the "Height" box, but not both.

In a 6" x 9" book with ¾" left and right margins, your images can be a maximum of 4 ½" wide if you want to keep them within the book's ¾" margins. When you enter a photo's width, its height will automatically adjust itself proportionately. But if the photo is a portrait or other tall photo, its height may be too tall at the 4 ½" width. In such cases, enter the height you want into the "height" box and let the width adjust itself.

Now click **OK** and your photo will shrink to the size you specified. On the top menu bar, click **View** and **Zoom In** several times to fill the screen with your photo.

And finally, now that we have your interior photo's resolution and size set, we'll change its color mode to *Grayscale*:

7. With your selected picture in the workspace, click **Image** on the top menu bar. On the drop-down menu, position your cursor over **Mode**. This brings up another drop-down menu to the right of "Mode." Its selections include "Bitmap," "Grayscale," "Indexed Color," and "RGB Color." Slide your cursor along "Mode" to the right and down the menu's options. You will see an arrow pointing to "RGB Color," the mode in which the scanner output the photo. Had your picture been in "Indexed Color" mode, the arrow on the menu would have pointed to "Indexed Color."

8. With your cursor on the "Mode" menu, click **Grayscale**. On the "ADOBE PHOTOSHOP ELEMENTS 9" dialog box that comes up, beneath "Discard color information?" click **OK.** This changes your photo's color mode from RGB or Indexed Color to Grayscale.

9. To Save your processed photo and preserve its original, click **File** on the menu bar at the top of your screen and then click **Save As.** In the SAVE AS dialog box that comes up, navigate to My Pictures or to the location you choose. Enter a file name that includes the word *processed*. Click the **arrow** at the right end of the "Format" window and select **JPEG** if it is not already there. Then click **Save**.

On the JPEG OPTION dialog box that comes up, under "Image Options," check to see that "Quality" **12**, and **Maximum** are selected. Under "Format Options," see that "Baseline" (**Standard**) is selected. Then click **OK** at the top of the box. Your *grayscale* photo has been saved and is now ready for insertion into your book block.

Processing Scanners' Images for Interior Pages
Your photos from your scanner should already be sized to fit on your book's pages, and you should have previously set their resolution to 300 dpi. However, their color mode must be changed to *Grayscale* if they are to be used inside your book. To do this, bring them into Photoshop Elements and follow Steps 7, 8 and 9 above.

Processing Color Images for Book Covers
For color photos to be inserted on covers, process them as per Steps 1 through 9, except in Step 8, click **RGB** for the color mode. Then **Save** them using **Save As** described in Step 9 above.

Enhancing Photos
If you want to edit the appearance of your photos, you can use Photoshop Elements' **Clone** tool to remove blemishes and

other undesirable elements. (See your Photoshop manual or **Help** to do this if you don't know how.)

But even if you don't want to edit your photos using the clone tool, you should at least adjust your interior photos' **Brightness** and/or **Contrast** to levels that will produce maximum quality when they are printed on a POD press. To do this, bring them into Photoshop and click **Enhance** on Photoshop's top tool bar.

On the dropdown menu that comes up, move your cursor down over **Adjust Lighting.** From the options presented, click either **Brightness/Contrast** or **Levels**. Use one or the other of these options, not both.

With **Brightness/Contrast** selected, in the dialog box that comes up, move each slider to produce the look you want. Then click **OK**. I strongly advise you to adjust your photos to look far brighter and less dark that you normally would choose to see them. Otherwise, they will look too dark in your book.

With **Levels** selected, you can adjust the "Input Levels" by clicking on and dragging the little arrows at the bottom of the graph. Moving the center arrow to the left produces the best results. Experiment with the left and right arrows. Again, I advise you to lighten your photos significantly. Then click **OK**.

After you have converted your *300 dpi* interior photos from *RGB* or *Indexed Color* mode to *Grayscale* mode, and you have done all the editing you intend to do on them and on your cover's color photos, save them again, using **Save As** described in Step 9 above. (You might want to create a new folder there and name it "My book's photos, processed and enhanced.") Enter a **file name** for whatever photo you are saving, select **JPEG** as the format type, and then click **Save**.

On the JPEG OPTION dialog box that comes up, under "Image Options," check to see that "Quality" **12**, and **Maximum** are selected. Under "Format Options," see that "Baseline" (**Standard**) is selected. Then click **OK** at the top of the box. Your *grayscale* photo has been saved and is now ready for insertion into your book block.

INSERTING YOUR IMAGES

A Few Notes before Inserting Images

1. Do not resize your images in Word. Use Photoshop as instructed above or use another image editing program to size the images for your book and then save them at 300 dpi resolution.

2. Your image insertion task will be easier if you insert each of your photos on a separate page without text, other than image captions. If you formatted your images *originally*— before you saved them—to fill the width of your pages (margin-to-margin), they should be the right size when you insert them.

3. As I said earlier, in a 6" x 9" book like this one, your images can be a maximum of 4 ½" wide if you want to keep them within the book's ¾" margins. When using photos with short heights, you can sometimes insert two, one above the other, on a single page. But don't let their heights, singly or combined, exceed about 6 ¼" or you won't have room for a caption or captions. When you get your photos

inserted, you can reduce their sizes slightly if you like, but don't enlarge them. (More about this later.)

4. If you are spacing your lines at anything above *single space*, you will have great difficulty inserting a photo if you do not, beforehand, go to the page on which you intend to insert your picture, click your cursor on the **line** at which you want the *top* of your photo to appear, and change *only* that line to **single** space. See instructions in "Inserting Your Images" below to reset this line to single space.

Inserting Your Images

1. **Open** your book block file to the first page on which you want to insert an image.
2. Click **File** at the left end of the top tool bar.
3. Click **Options** at the bottom of the menu that drops down.
4. On the WORD OPTIONS dialog box that comes up, on the left side of the box, click **Advanced**.
5. On the right side of the box, scroll down to the heading "Image Size and Quality."
6. Put a check in the **box** to the left of "Do not compress images in file." Then click **OK** at the bottom of the box. THIS MUST BE DONE BEFORE INSERTING IMAGES!!!
7. If you haven't already done so, click your cursor on the **line** at which you want the *top* of your photo to appear and change *only* that line to **Single** space. To reset that line to single space, click the **Home** tab, and in the "Paragraph" group, click the **Line and Paragraph Spacing** icon and select **1.0** on the dropdown menu. This change will affect only that line.

8. Back on your book block file, click the **Insert** tab on the upper tool bar.
9. In the "Illustrations" group, click **Picture**.
10. In the INSERT PICTURE dialog box that comes up, navigate to the 300 dpi picture you want to insert and **select** its file (don't open it) with one click only.
11. Click **Insert** at the bottom of the box. Your image will appear with its top at the line on which your cursor is clicked.
12. **Repeat** steps 7 through 11 for every other image you insert in your book block. To insert an image on your book's cover, click your cursor on the cover where you want the top of the image to appear and **repeat** steps 2 through 11.

This sequence of steps will make possible the converting of your book block file to PDF without Word's reducing your images' 300 dpi resolutions. And, when converting your Word files to PDF using Adobe Acrobat, DO NOT USE "SAVE AS" on the File menu. Follow my instructions carefully in chapter 10, "Converting Your Word Files To PDF With Adobe Acrobat." If you use another PDF conversion program, follow its instructions.

If you wish to drag a photo to a position other than where your cursor's placement located it, you must first click on the photo to bring up the "Picture Tools" and "Format" tabs. Click the **Format** tab to be sure its menu is active. In the "Arrange" group, click **Wrap Text** and then click **Top and Bottom** on the dropdown menu. Now you can click on the photo and drag it where you want it.

I must also inform you that inserting any image will push down whatever line, block of lines, or text that follows the image. You will have to **Delete** those added blank lines to bring the text back up to its original position. If you left an entire page blank on which to insert your photo, you will have to delete an entire page of blank lines beneath the photo to bring your text back up to the top of the page following the photo.

Sizing Your Inserted Images

Once you get your 300 dpi photo inserted into your book block, you can make it smaller, if you like. Click anywhere on it and the "Picture Tools" and "Format" tabs will appear on the top menu bar. Click the **Format** tab beneath "Picture Tools" if the "Size" group does not appear in the upper, right corner of the "Format" tab's menu. Then in the "Size" group, enter your changes in *either* the picture's Height *or* its Width. Press **Enter** on your keyboard. Your photo will shrink to the size you entered.

Placing Borders around Your Images

Click anywhere on your image and the "Picture Tools" and "Format" tabs will appear. Click the **Format** tab to be sure its menu is active. Now click **Picture Border** in the "Picture Styles" group. Slide your cursor down to **Weight** and then over to the list of weights to the right. Move your cursor over your choice of line weight for the border around your image and click that **weight**. Clicking on the line weight closes the dialog box, so you will have to click **Picture Border** again to select a different line weight.

If you want a colored border for your cover photo, click **Picture Border** again and click the **color** you want. Click outside the photo to clear it.

OTHER COMMENTS CONCERNING IMAGES

You may enter a caption beneath each interior image as you insert it. If you mess up a photo, click on it, press **Delete** on your keyboard, and then re-insert it.

When you finish inserting all your interior images, be sure to make another **Save As** template and name it "3. Book Block with Images."

To insert color images onto your book's cover, follow the procedure described above and see chapter 9, "Creating Your Book's Cover."

Be sure to follow my instructions carefully on page 34 under "Inserting Your Images." Unless you do exactly as instructed in steps 1 through 6, Word will arbitrarily reduce the resolution of your 300 dpi photos and images to 199 dpi. As I have previously told you, CreateSpace (and probably other self-publishing firms) requires 300 dpi for all images inserted.

There is more yet to do concerning the processing of your interior photos, but I will cover this in chapter 10, "Converting Your Word Files to PDF with Adobe Acrobat."

Chapter Five

INSERTING SECTION BREAKS

Headers and Footers can contain page numbers as well as textual headings. To insert page numbers and text into headers and footers, you must know *where* and *how* to insert section breaks. Without this knowledge, you will run into a mental wall when you try to insert page numbers and text in a manner specified by *The Chicago Manual of Style*.

GENERAL INFORMATION ON SECTION BREAKS

Basically, a section break affects only the page numbers and text headings you place inside *header* and *footer* boxes. You normally don't see these dash-lined boxes at the tops and bottoms of your pages unless you access and enable **Insert Header** or **Footer** commands. However, even though you don't see these boxes, their contents (if any) are dimly visible on your manuscript and do print along with the rest of your book's text. Nothing is visible and nothing prints, of course, if you insert nothing into your header and footer boxes.

Although you *can* insert page numbers and text headings without first inserting section breaks, your efforts will be extremely limited. For example, with no section breaks, every page in your book will be able to display only visible, sequential numbers of only one type (Roman or Arabic numbers or alphabet letters). And, you will have only one text heading that you can insert in "Even Page" headers and one different heading in "Odd Page" headers. Anything you write inside an odd page header box will appear in the odd page header of every odd page in your entire book (except the first page, on which its appearance can be made optional). The same will be true for even page headers.

To avoid these limitations that prevent you from placing *different* header text in *different* headers throughout your book, you must first insert section breaks between many elements and parts of your book and then unlink the headers in each section from those in sections preceding and following each section. And, if you are inserting "drop folios" (numbers at the bottoms of your pages), and you want to change from Roman numerals for your front matter to Arabic numbers for your text, you must also unlink your footers at that junction.

Also, if you want to insert photos, illustrations, or other images on pages that need to be without *visible* page numbers and without header text, you must bracket such pages with section breaks before and after.

"OK," you are probably saying, "I get it! I must use section breaks, but you still haven't told me what they are or how I can insert them."

OK, I'm getting to that. To sum up, a section break is used to isolate the headers and footers on a group of pages (or those on a single page) from the headers and footers on all other pages in *preceding* sections. As previously stated, this isolation allows you to insert different types of page numbers or different header text in different parts of your book.

Although you *can* insert section breaks as you write your book, it is best to wait until your manuscript is finished, with all images inserted if you have any. Then you can insert your breaks all at the same time.

First, I will tell you *where* to insert section breaks, and then I will tell you *how* to insert them.

WHERE TO INSERT SECTION BREAKS

To help you visualize these section break locations, I have prepared the chart you will see on the next page. (In the next chapter, I will explain the chart's placement of page numbers.)

Please bear in mind that although this chart will probably match the pages of your own book down to the beginning of the "Contents" pages, you may have fewer or even more pages than I show in the Contents and sections following. Use the chart only as a guide for inserting breaks in your book.

I have placed the chart on two separate pages so that you can scan and print it and refer to it when reading my instructions on where and how to insert section breaks and page numbers.

REFERENCE CHART FOR BREAKS AND PAGE NUMBERS
(Your own book may differ.)

Actual Page	Given Num.	Visible Num.	Book Element	Section Breaks
1	i	-	1st Half Title	
2	ii	-	Blank (you insert)	
3	iii	-	Full Title	
4	iv	-	Copyright	
5	v	-	Dedication	1ST Break to **Section 2**, next odd (right)
6	vi	-	Blank Ø	
7	vii	-	Contents-1	
8	viii	viii	Contents-2	
9	ix	ix	Contents-3	
10	x	x	Contents-4	2nd Break to **Section 3**, next odd (right)
11	xi	-	Introduction-1	
12	xii	xii	Introduction-2	3rd Break to **Section 4**, next odd (right)
13	1	-	2nd Half Title	4th Break to **Section 5**, next odd (right)
14	2	-	Blank Ø	
15	3	-	Chap 1-1	
16	4	4	Chap 1-2	
17	5	5	Chap 1-3	5th Break to **Section 6**, next odd (right)
18	6	-	Blank Ø	
19	7	-	Chap 2-1	
20	8	8	Chap 2-2	
21	9	9	Chap 2-3	6th Break to **Section 7**, next odd (right)

Actual Page	Given Num.	Visible Num.	Book Element	Section Breaks
151	139	139	Chap xx-last page	Break to **Section nn,** next odd (right)
152	140	-	Blank Ø	
153	141	-	Bibliography	Break to **Section nn,** next odd(right)
154	142	-	Blank Ø	
155	143	-	Index-1-1	
156	144	144	Index-1-2	

Notes on Chart:
Under "Visible Num." column, all pages are counted, but only those indicated have visible numbers.

Underlined "Book Element" pages have section breaks inserted at bottoms of those pages.

Book Element pages labeled "Blank Ø" are those inserted by Word to insure that next sections begin on desired odd pages. You will not be able to write on these "Blank Ø" pages, but your POD printer will issue them as real, blank pages.

Here are the locations in your book that require the insertion of section breaks. (Use the chart as a reference only. Your book may differ.)

1. Your *first* section break must be inserted at the *bottom* of the page immediately *preceding* the *first* page of your "Contents." This is usually the page containing the "Dedication." If you have "Acknowledgments" on page 6, Word will not insert a blank page for page 6, and your first break will be at the *bottom* of that page. If you have no "Dedication" and no "Acknowledgments," you will need to place your first break at the bottom of the "Copyright" page.

     This first break is placed here to isolate all the headers and footers above it so that no header text or page numbers will appear in them.

2. Your *second* break must be inserted at the *bottom* of the *last* page of your "Contents." If your "Contents" has only one page, insert the second break at the bottom of that single page. This last page of "Contents" *precedes* the first page of your "Introduction," "Preface," or other introductory element. If you have no "Introduction," the last page of your "Contents" *precedes* your one-page 2nd Half Title.

3. Your *third* break must be inserted at the *bottom* of the *last* page of your "Introduction." This last page of your "Introduction" *precedes* your one-page 2nd Half Title. If you have no "Introduction," the break at the *bottom* of the *last* page of your "Contents" *precedes* your one-page 2nd Half Title.

4. Your *fourth* break must be inserted at the *bottom* of your single-page 2nd Half Title. This page *precedes* either your *first* "Part" page (if you have one) or the *first* page of your "Chapter 1" as shown in the chart.

5. Your *fifth* break must be inserted either at the *bottom* of your first "Part" page, or at the *bottom* of the *last* page of your "Chapter 1" as shown in the chart.

6. From here throughout the rest of your book, insert a section break at the *bottom* of the page immediately *preceding* the *first* page of each chapter, the *bottom* of the page *preceding* each "Part" page (if any), and the *bottom* of the page *preceding* each element of back matter.

7. In addition to the above locations, you must also bracket with breaks all pages containing photos or other images on which you don't want header text or page numbers to appear. For each such page, a break must be inserted at the *bottom* of the page *preceding* the image, followed by a break at the *bottom* of the page on which the image is placed.

HOW TO INSERT SECTION BREAKS

Each time you insert a section break, you will have to specify whether you want the new section to start on the next **Even Page**, or the next **Odd Page**. (We will not be using the "Next Page" or the "Continuous" page options.)

And—unless you specify otherwise—that first page of the new section (whether it is "Even," or "Odd") will have a header named "First Page Header" and a footer named "First Page Footer." This is because you checked the box for **Different first page** way back there when you were doing your "Page Setup." You did this in order to insure that the first page of each chapter and the first page of other elements in your book could remain without text or number in its header and, on some pages, its footer.

A "Different first page," of course, can be either an even-numbered (left) page or an odd-numbered (right) page. The page following a "Different first page" can also be Even or Odd, depending on whether that "Different first page" was Even or Odd.

When you include photos and/or other images in your book block, inserting section breaks becomes more complicated, but don't let this deter you. I will tell you how to do it. But first, let's consider inserting breaks in books *without* images. (Read the following section even though your book has images.)

Books *without* Images

Bring up your "2. Book Block" template. Make a **Save As** copy and name it "4. Book Block with Section Breaks." (No, I didn't make a mistake. I said name it "4" because "3" has images.)

To begin this procedure, scroll to the *bottom* of the page immediately *preceding* the *first* page of your "Contents." (This is usually a "Dedication.") Click your cursor at the end of, or (preferably) anywhere below, the last line of text on that page.

Inserting Section Breaks

In the "Paragraph" group under the **Home** tab, click the **Show/Hide** button. (Unless you do this, you will not be able to see the section break you are about to insert.)

Click the **Page Layout** tab on the top menu bar. In the "Page Setup" group, click **Breaks**. On the dialog box that drops down, under the "Section Breaks" options, click **Odd Page.**

You have just inserted your first section break. The break will show up as a double row of dotted lines labeled "Section Break (Odd Page)." This means that you want your text to appear on the very next odd page. Had you selected **Even Page** for the break, it would be labeled "Section Break (Even Page)."

Additional Notes

1. Select **Even Page** if you want text to appear on the next even (left) page. If the page you have your cursor on is even, Word will insert a blank, odd page between it and the next even page.

2. Select **Odd Page** if you want text to appear on the next odd (right) page. If the page you have your cursor on is odd, Word will insert a blank, even page between it and the next odd page.

3. To delete a section break, click the **Show/Hide** button, click your cursor on the double-dotted **break line** (or at end of the last line on the page if the break line is not visible), and click **Delete** on your keyboard. If you do this, the two sections previously separated will become one,

sharing whatever formatting is contained in the *bottom* section.

4. To change a section's starting page (odd or even), click your cursor on the double-dotted **Section Break line** (or at end of the last line on the page if the break line is not visible) and click **Delete** on your keyboard. Go back to the insertion procedure above and, under the "Section Breaks" options, click **Even Page** or **Odd Page.**

5. When you insert a section break, that break pushes all the blank lines beneath it (including the line your cursor was on) down to the next page, thereby shifting text on that page down that many lines. To remove those added blank lines on the next page, click your cursor on the top line of that page and click **Delete** on your keyboard repeatedly until the text beneath it returns to its former position.

6. If a section break that is inserted on the very *bottom* line of a page is at the end a *full line* of text, dashed lines indicating a section break there will not be visible, but a change in section numbers can be seen by clicking Word's **Insert** tab and then, in the "Header & Footer" group, click **Header**. At the bottom of the BUILT-IN dialog box, click **Edit Header**. Now you can see the dashed header lines and the section number at the top of the page.

   (Clicking **Edit Header** or **Header and Footer** always returns you to the header of the page your cursor is clicked on, so remember to click on the page containing the section break you want to see. Otherwise, Word will return you to the page your cursor was last clicked on—and you will have to scroll up or down to the page you want to see.)

7. If your section break is on an odd (right) page, and you want the first page of the following section to appear on an odd (right) page, Word will insert one blank, even (left) page on which a page number will not be visible, and on which no header or footer will appear. Even-to-even pages get an odd page inserted between them. These added pages appear only on **Print Preview**, but your POD printer will issue them as real, blank pages. To access **Print Preview,** click **File** then **Print**. The page you are currently viewing will appear on the right side of your screen. Move the **Zoom** slider at the bottom, right of your screen to the left of 100% to see multiple pages.

8. If your book is non-fiction, (excluding autobiography or memoir), and it has no images in its interior, you will always select **Odd page** for each "Section start." For fiction, autobiography, and memoir books, you may start the first page of each of your chapters on the page that follows the last page of the previous chapter, whether Odd or Even.

Books *with* Images
Bring up your "3. Book Block with Images" template. Follow the same procedure specified above for books *without* images but include the following changes:

As before stated, all photos or other images on pages by themselves must be *enclosed* within their own sections (a section break at the *bottom* of the page *preceding* each photo and a section break at the *bottom* of the page containing each photo). This will make the page immediately *following* each photo become a "Different first page" since that page begins a new section. (You initially specified that all *first* pages of all sections be made "Different first page.")

You will have to change this for each section that immediately *follows* a page on which a photo was inserted *if that photo page was inserted between pages of text within a chapter.* If you interrupt the flow of your chapter's text by inserting a page on which *only* a photo appears (a page on which you want no header text or visible page number to appear), the section break at the *bottom* of the photo's page will automatically start the next section with a "First Page Header." But, you will *want* the page of text following the photo to resume its header text and visible page number. Therefore you would delete the "Different first page" specification *for this section.*

To do this, click your cursor at the top of the page that follows the section break you want to change and then click the **Insert** tab. In the "Header & Footer" group, click **Header** and then **Edit Header**. This will bring up the "Header & Footer Tools" and "Design" tabs. In the "Options" group, **deselect** the checkmark (click on it) in the box to the left of "Different first page." Look at the header box and see that it has changed from "First Page Header" to "Even Page Header" or "Odd Page Header." (This change affects *only* this section.)

Now that you know where and how to insert section breaks, go through your entire book and insert them everywhere they are needed. (Refer to "Reference Chart for Breaks and Page Numbers" on page 42.) **Save** your work.

UNLINKING SECTIONS

When first inserted, a section break, by default, does *not* isolate all the headers or footers on that section's pages from all the headers or footers in the section *preceding* that section. First Page Headers in the newly inserted section remain linked to First Page Headers in the section immediately *preceding* that section, Even Page Headers remain linked to Even Page Headers in the *preceding* section, and Odd Page Headers remain linked to Odd Page Headers. The same is true for the section immediately *following* the new section, provided the following section has not been *unlinked*.

If left as is, this default, *linked* condition will cause all sections' First Page Headers to share the content of any First Page Header you write something in, and all section's First Page Footers to share the content of any First Page Footer you write in. Even Page Headers and Footers and Odd Page Headers and Footers will share their content similarly. For example, the words "Chapter One," when written in an Odd Page Header, will appear in all Odd Page Headers on all the odd pages of your book (except those blank pages Word inserts). This default condition can be changed by *unlinking* section breaks in appropriate, key positions.

To begin unlinking your book's sections, bring up your "4. Book Block with Section Breaks" and make a **Save As** template named "5. Book Block with Unlinked Section Breaks." Click *on* the **Show/Hide** button, then click your cursor anywhere on the page immediately *following* your *first* section break. On the chart, this is actual page 7 (vii), the first page of your "Contents."

With your cursor clicked anywhere at the top of the page immediately *following* your first section break, click the **Insert** tab. In the "Header & Footer" group, click **Header**. At the bottom of the BUILT-IN dialog box that comes up, click **Edit Header**. Now you can see the Header and Footer boxes at the top and bottom of the page you are on. This also brings up the "Header & Footer Tools" and "Design" tabs on the top tool bar.

Notice that this header containing your cursor is labeled "First Page Header-Section 2." This is because, way back in chapter 1 when you were doing your book's page setup, you selected **Different first page** for your Headers and Footers. This selection allows you to leave any section's First Page Header *without* header text and page number.

In the "Navigation" group, position your cursor over the **icon** that reads **Link to Previous** and click it. You will see that, on the right end of the header, the little shaded box containing the words "Same as Previous" has disappeared. (This disappearing indicator gives quick, visual proof that a section's header or footer has been unlinked.) You have just unlinked your First Page Header *in this section* from the First Page Header in the section *preceding* this section.

Now scroll down one page to the next page, labeled "Even Page Header." Click your cursor *inside* the header on that page. Again, click the **icon** in the "Navigation" group that reads **Link to Previous**. You have just unlinked all of your Even Page Headers *in this section* from all the Even Page Headers in the section *preceding* this section.

Scroll down one page to the next page, labeled "Odd Page Header." Click your cursor inside this header and unlink it just as you unlinked the Even Page Header above. You have just unlinked all of your Odd Page Headers *in this section* from all the Odd Page Headers in the section *preceding* this section.

You need not unlink the odd and even headers remaining (if any) *in this section*. Unlinking just the three headers above unlinks all of them. But you have *not* unlinked all these headers from those headers in the sections *following* this section.

To unlink all the headers in Section 2 from those following in Section 3, you must repeat the above procedure for Section 3. But before continuing to unlink headers beyond Section 2, read the section below:

TO UNLINK OR NOT TO UNLINK?

As you have discovered by unlinking the headers on the first three pages of Section 2, unlinking headers is not all that difficult, nor is unlinking footers. Ah, but the real problem is deciding *which* headers and footers should be unlinked and *which* headers and footers should remain linked.

At this point I must advise you that there are *two* ways of solving this problem. There is the easy but time-consuming way or the more complex but faster way. Read my instructions for using each of these methods and then decide which you want to follow.

Method 1: The Easy But Time-Consuming Way

Doing it this way is a no-brainer. You simply unlink *every* First Page Header, *every* Even Page Header, and *every* Odd Page Header in *every* section throughout your book. If you plan to use drop folios (numbers at the bottoms of your pages), also unlink each section's footers. This insures that *every* section's headers and footers are isolated from those of *all* other *preceding* and *following* sections. This also relieves you of having to decide what to unlink and what to leave linked.

"Well, that's not so bad," you say. "After all, I will only have to unlink the headers and footers on the First Page, the first Even Page, and the first Odd Page in each section."

You are right, but that's not *all* you have to do. With no Even Page headers linked, none can copy the text you will enter in the headers above them. When you enter the title of your book in the first Even Page Header of Section 2, the Even Page Headers in Section 3 will not duplicate your book's title. Nor will any Even Page Header following Section 3 do it. You will have to enter your book's title in the first Even Page Header in *every* section in your book. You will have to enter your page numbers the same way.

Even so, this *is* the easiest way to do it. (I used this method for my first book, until I learned the faster way.) But first, try the more complex unlinking procedure below. Then when you begin inserting your page numbers and header text as per the instructions in the next two chapters, if you can't seem to make it work for you, come back here and unlink your headers and footers this easy way.

Method 2: The More Complex but Faster Way
To explain how to use this method, I will describe what must be done with each of three kinds of headers.

First Page Headers

As before stated, the purpose of using a "Different first page" header is that of isolating the header of the first page of a section from the headers on all the other pages *in that section.* Since you want nothing to appear in your First Page Header, you can simply leave it blank, with no entry, and whatever you write in that section's following Odd and Even headers will not appear in your First Page Header.

In fact, even though I just instructed you (as an exercise) to unlink the First Page Header on the first page of your Contents, you need not unlink *any* of the rest of your First Page Headers in *any* of the sections throughout your book. This is because you will never write anything in any of your First Page Headers. And, since any and all First Page Headers will remain blank, the "Same as previous" format for all *linked* First Page Headers will have nothing to copy.

As you proceed with this unlinking procedure, check to see that the header on the first page of each section is, in fact, labeled "First Page Header." If it is labeled "Odd Page Header" or "Even Page Header," change it to "First Page Header" as follows:

Click your cursor inside the header on the page you want to change. In the "Options" group under the "Header & Footer Tools" and "Design" tabs, click the box for **Different First Page.** The header changes to "First Page Header." This will change *only* the first page *in that section.*

The exception to starting a section with a "Different first page" (First Page Header) is where a section break is at the bottom of a photo page that is inserted *between* two pages of text. In this case, use the above procedure to ***deselect*** "First

Page Header" (remove the check mark in its box), thereby changing it to "Odd Page Header" or "Even Page Header."

Even Page Headers

If you are using Roman numerals to number your front matter pages (as per *The Chicago Manual of Style*), you *must* unlink your Even Page Headers in all sections down to and including the first Even Page Header in Section 5. On the chart, this is the Even Page Header on actual page 16.

Then, if you are inserting the title of your book in all Even Page Headers throughout the rest of your book, you can leave all following Even Page Headers *linked*, beginning with the first Even Page Header in Section 6 on actual page 20.

If you were to unlink *all* Even Page Headers, your header insertions would still work, but you would have to re-enter the page number and title of your book in the first Even Page Header of each section throughout your book.

Odd Page Headers

Because Odd Page headers are normally used to display *different* text for each chapter or other elements in your book (Chapter One, Chapter Two, Bibliography, etc.), you *must* unlink *all* of your Odd Page Headers throughout your book. This means, of course, unlinking only the *first* Odd Page Header in each section.

To Sum Up

To unlink your headers as described above, here are the headers you must **unlink**:

First Page Headers: None

Even Page Headers: Only those on the chart's actual pages 8, 12, & 16 (the *first* Even Page headers in sections 2, 3, & 5)

Odd Page Headers: All

If you want to use *drop folios* to number your pages, here are the footers you must unlink:

First Page Footer on actual page 7, Section 2
First Page Footer on actual page 11, Section 3
First Page Footer on actual page 13, Section 4
First Page Footer on actual page 15, Section 5

First Even Page Footer on actual page 8, Section 2
First Odd Page Footer on actual page 9, Section 2
First Even Page Footer on actual page 12, Section 3
First Even Page Footer on actual page 16, Section 5
First Odd Page Footer on actual page 17, Section 5

Now go ahead and unlink the specified headers (and footers, if you want drop folios) in all the sections throughout your book.

To restore an unlinked header or footer to a linked condition, just click your cursor inside that header or footer and then click the "Same as Previous" **icon** on the tool bar. On the box that comes up, click **Yes**.

Anytime you want to exit the Header & Footer view, just double-click anywhere on that page's text (not inside the header) or click **Close Header and Footer** in the "Close" box on the right end of the menu bar.

After you have finished unlinking the above-specified pages in all your book's sections, **Save** your "5. Book Block with Unlinked Section Breaks" for later use.

Chapter Six

INSERTING PAGE NUMBERS

Inserting page numbers can become difficult and frustrating until you learn exactly how to do it. The complexity of this task varies with your book's design.

Inserting numbers is simple and easy if all you want to do is number your pages from start to finish with one type of number (Roman, Arabic, or alphabet letter), with every page getting a *visible* number except those blank pages added by Word. Today's major style guides, however, do not approve of numbering a book's pages this way.

Many publishers today still follow the page-numbering style set by *The Chicago Manual of Style*. Alternately, some modern-day authors have dispensed with using Roman numerals for front matter before switching to Arabic numbers for their text. Some begin by numbering the first page of their books (the first half title page) with an invisible *Arabic* number "1" and continue by consecutively numbering all following pages with visible and invisible *Arabic* numbers. And some leave their front matter entirely without page numbers and begin numbering their text with an invisible *Arabic* number "1" on the 2nd half title page or an invisible *Arabic* "1" on the first page of chapter one. And, instead of invisible numbers on some pages, some authors insert visible "drop folios" on them (numbers at the bottoms of pages).

After you learn to insert your page numbers as per *The Chicago Manual of Style*, I'm sure you'll be able to insert them any *other* way you want.

INSERTING PAGE NUMBERS AS PER
THE CHICAGO MANUAL OF STYLE

What do you do if you want the page numbers on some pages in your book to be invisible, but you still want those pages to be counted? The first thing you must do, of course, is to decide which pages you *don't* want visible numbers on. According to *The Chicago Manual of Style*, these are the pages that should have *invisible* page numbers:

Pages That Require Invisible Numbers
All blank pages
First half title (contains only the book's main title)
Title page (book's title, subtitle, author's name, and publisher)
Copyright page (may include acknowledgments)
Dedication
Epigraph (if any)
First page of the following: table of contents, foreword, preface, introduction, or prologue (Exception: drop folios are acceptable on the first pages of these sections.)
Second half title
Part titles (if any)
First page of each chapter (A drop folio is also OK here.)
Pages containing *only* illustrations, photos, or tables (all these with or without captions)
First page of each section in back matter (A drop folio is OK.)

A Return to the Chart of Breaks & Page Numbers

Get out your scanned copy of the "Breaks and Page Numbers" chart you used as a reference during reading the previous chapter. (If you don't have a scanned copy, refer to this chart in the previous chapter.) In this chart, I show at a glance which pages of a book should be visibly numbered and which pages should be counted but left without visible numbers. This chart follows conventions set by *The Chicago Manual of Style*. Though drop folios are permissible, I did not use them in my chart.

In your own book, use drop folios if you like. Personally, I prefer drop folios, at least on first pages of chapters and some other book sections. (You may use a combination of header-placed page numbers *and* drop folios.) It seems rather puzzling to me that some books' tables of contents list chapter one, chapter two, etc. as beginning on pages such-and-such, but you can find no numbers on those pages. I have placed all page numbers in *this* book at the tops of their pages because I wanted you to be able to see this method of number placement.

Before beginning to insert page numbers, make a **Save As** copy of your "5. Book Block with Unlinked Section Breaks" template. Name this new template "6. Book Block with Page Numbers."

And, perhaps this tip will keep you sane during your number-insertion process: After you successfully complete your insertion of page numbers in *each* section, click the **Save** icon on your tool bar. That way, if you mess up the next section's insertions—or if you run into a stubborn problem and you want to start over—you can just **Close** your file without saving it and then reopen it at your last **Save** point.

Inserting Page Numbers

Since all "First Page Headers" will be left blank (including those on one-page book elements), we will begin inserting page numbers in the first multi-page section's first "Even Page Header."

Inserting Even Numbers in Section 2

To begin your even number insertions, scroll down to the second page of your "Contents" (actual page 8 on the chart, the first even-numbered page in section 2) and click your cursor anywhere on that page. In the **Home** tab's "Paragraph" group, click *on* the **Show/Hide** button. In the **Insert** tab's "Header & Footer" group, click **Header**, then **Edit Header** at the bottom of the BUILT-IN dialog box that comes up. The "Header & Footer Tools" and "Design" tabs come up activated on the top menu bar. In the "Header & Footer" group, click **Page Number**. In the dropdown menu that comes up, click **Format Page Numbers**.

In the PAGE NUMBER FORMAT dialog box that comes up, click the arrow on the "Number format" window and select **i, ii, iii**. Under "Page numbering," select **Start at**. Roman number **i** will appear in the window. Enter **vi** (*see notes below) or click the arrow to bring **vi** up in the window. Then click **OK**.

Notice that Word has returned your cursor to the First Page Header just above the page you were on. Scroll back down to that first Even Page Header and click your cursor inside the header.

Notes before continuing procedure:

The following instructions assume that your book elements match those on my chart. If your book differs, you will have to figure out what number you should insert in the "Start at" box.

Since your cursor is clicked on an Even page, you are inserting numbers *only* for the *even* numbered pages. Therefore this "Start at" Roman **vi** is the number of the *first* even numbered page in this Section, which number is the number of the blank page that Word has inserted following the break on page 5.

To verify this, look at the chart and you will see that the first page *following* section break 1 is, in fact, page 6 (**vi**), a blank, even-numbered page that Word has inserted in order to place the first page of "Contents" on recto page 7. The next *even* numbered page is **viii**, the number you want to appear in the header on the page your cursor is clicked on.

If you have no "Dedication," your first section break will be at the *bottom* of page 4 (**iv**), your "Copyright" page. In this case, since page 4 is an even number, Word will not have to insert a blank page to insure that Contents-1 will be on a recto page 5, numbered with invisible **v**. Therefore you would insert **v** in your page numbering "Start at" window. This would number your first even-numbered page **vi.**

Now, to continue the insertion procedure, in the "Header & Footer" group, you must click **Page Number** again. On the dropdown menu that comes up, move your cursor over "Top of Page" and click **Plain Number 1**, the top option in the "Simple" box. Roman numeral **viii** (or the number for this page in your own book) now appears in the header at its left end.

If you scroll down two pages to the next *even* page in this section, you will find its header numbered with the next *even* Roman numeral, **x**. Even numbers will also appear sequentially on all other even pages you might have *in this section*.

Inserting Odd Numbers in Section 2

Now scroll back up one page to actual page 9, the first Odd Page in this section, and click your cursor *inside* its header. Under the "Header & Footer Tools" and "Design" tabs, in the "Header & Footer" group, click **Page Number**. This time, move your cursor over **Top of Page** instead of clicking "Format Page Numbers." Click **Plain Number 3** on the "Simple" dropdown menu. Roman number **ix** will appear in the header at its right end.

In your own book, if you have more odd pages in this section, odd numbers will also appear sequentially on all the remaining odd pages *in this section*.

At any time you wish to do so, you can select the position in your headers that you want your numbers to appear. Click your cursor inside the header you want to change and then click the **Home** tab. In the "Paragraph" group, click the **Align Left**, **Center**, or **Align Right** button. Or, click the **Insert** tab and, in the "Header & Footer" group, click **Page Number.** In the dialog box that comes up, position your cursor over **Top of Page** and click one of the **Plain Number** options for left, center, or right positions.

Inserting Even Numbers in Section 3

When you get past your "Contents" pages, click your cursor inside the header on the second page of your "Introduction."

In the "Header & Footer" group, under the "Header & Footer Tools" and "Design" tabs, click **Page Number** and then click **Format Page Numbers.** In the PAGE NUMBER FORMAT dialog box that comes up, click the arrow for "Number format" and select **i, ii, iii**. Then click **Continue from previous** and **OK**.

Note that Word has returned your cursor to the First Page Header. Scroll back down one page to the first Even Page Header and click your cursor inside it. (*Be sure to watch for this as you proceed to number your pages!*) Then click **Page Number** again, move your cursor over **Top of Page**, and click **Plain Number 1** on the dropdown menu. Roman number **xii**, (or the number for your book's page) will appear in the left end of the header box.

Inserting NO *Numbers in One-Page Sections*
If your "Contents" or your "Introduction" has only *one* page, that page's header will be labeled "First Page Header." In this case—and for all other one-page sections with a First Page Header (including pages for photos and other graphics)— enter *nothing* in that header, bypass that section, and go on to the next section following it or to the next section with two or more pages.

Continuing Your Page Number Insertions
When you get down to your 2nd Half Title page, leave its header blank and go on to the *second* page of "Chapter 1," the first page labeled "Even Page Header" in section 5. Click your cursor in that header and then click **Page Number** and **Format Page Numbers**. Select **1, 2, 3** for "Number

Format." Then select **Start at**, enter Arabic **2** in the window, and click **OK**.

But before clicking **Page Number** again to insert the number, notice that Word has again returned your cursor to the First Page Header. Scroll back down one page to the first Even Page Header and click your cursor inside it. Now click **Page Number** and move your cursor over **Top of Page**. In the "Simple" dropdown menu, click **Plain Number 1** and Arabic **4** will appear in the header of the first even page in this section.

Scroll down one page to the next page labeled "Odd Page Header" and click your cursor inside its header. Click **Page Number** again and then move your cursor over **Top of Page**, *not* "Format Page Numbers." On the "Simple" menu, click **Plain Number 3**. Arabic **5** will appear at the right end of the header box.

Continue your numbering procedure, but in this section and in all sections thereafter, the *even* page numbers should now automatically appear on all the remaining *even* pages. This is because, from this point on, all even pages remain *linked*, causing each section's even pages to copy the header text in the section's even pages above.

But since all Odd Page headers have been *unlinked*, you will have to insert all remaining odd page numbers in the first Odd Page Header of each remaining section in your book. To do this, all you need to do is to click your cursor in the *first* Odd Page Header of each section, click **Page Number**, move your cursor over **Top of Page**, and select **Plain Number 3**.

INSERTING PAGE NUMBERS YOUR OWN WAY

To begin implementing this "modern" method of numbering your pages, insert your *first* section break at the bottom of the last page of your front matter (Actual page 12 on my chart). Insert all other breaks following this one as prescribed in the previous chapter.

Then go to the page immediately *following* your 2nd Half Title (Actual page 15 on the chart) and apply to this section the same page numbering procedures you used above.

You may choose to count, invisibly in Arabic, the front matter pages and continue that count on into your text with visible Arabic numbers starting on the second page of your "Chapter 1." Or, if you want your front matter pages *not* to be counted, and you want your text to begin with a visible Arabic **4** on the second page of your "Chapter 1," simply enter Arabic **2** in the page numbering "Start at" box. Then continue as if you were formatting per *The Chicago Manual of Style* method of page numbering.

WRAPPING IT UP

Inserting Drop Folios
If you want to insert your page numbers at the bottoms of your pages, you should first unlink **footers** in the following places, their locations being referenced to my chart:
 First Page Footer on actual page 7, Section 2
 First Page Footer on actual page 11, Section 3
 First Page Footer on actual page 13, Section 4
 First Page Footer on actual page 15, Section 5

First Even Page Footer on actual page 8, Section 2
First Odd Page Footer on actual page 9, Section 2
First Even Page Footer on actual page 12, Section 3
First Even Page Footer on actual page 16, Section 5
First Odd Page Footer on actual page 17, Section 5

Although you *do* want *visible* page numbers to appear at the bottoms of the first pages of all chapters and some other book elements containing text, you *do not* want page numbers to appear at the bottoms of "Part" pages and pages on which *only* photos and/or other images appear. Therefore, you must *unlink* all First Page **Footers** on all such pages.

If you have no "Part" pages or images in your book, you may leave *linked* all First Page Footers *following* those shown above.

After unlinking your footers as described above, you are ready to insert page numbers into your footers. With your cursor clicked on the **first page** of your "Contents" (actual page 7 on the chart), click **Insert**. In the "Header & Footer" group, click **Footer**, not "Header," and then click **Edit Footer** at the bottom of the BUILT-IN dialog box. (Your cursor will appear inside the "First Page Footer, Section 2.") With the "Header & Footer Tools" and "Design" tabs activated, click **Page Number** in the "Header & Footer" group. Then click **Format Page Numbers** on the drop-down menu.

In the PAGE NUMBER FORMAT dialog box, in the "Number Format" window, select **i**, **ii**, **iii**. Under "Page Numbering," click **Start At** and enter Roman numeral **vi**. Now click **OK**.

Now click **Page Number** in the "Header & Footer" group, position your cursor over **Bottom of Page**, and click either **Plain Number 2** (center) or **Plain Number 3** (right). Roman numeral **vii** should appear in the footer.

To insert *even* and *odd* page numbers in Section 2, you won't have to click "Format Page Numbers." Since you have already specified the format for the *First Page Footer*, all you have to do to insert *odd* and *even* numbers is to click your cursor inside an *odd* or *even* **Footer**, click **Page Number** in the "Header & Footer" group, move your cursor over **Bottom of Page**, and click whatever position you want.

And, note that when you click **Page Number** to insert numbers on pages *following* the First Page, Word does *not* return your cursor to the First Page.

Now click your cursor inside **First Page Footer, Section 3** (actual page 11) and click **Page Number** and **Format Page Numbers**. Select **i, ii, iii** and **Continue from previous section** and click **OK**. Now click **Page Number** and under "Bottom of Page," click the **position** you want. Roman numeral **xi** will appear in the footer.

Now click your cursor inside **First Page Footer, Section 5** (actual page 15) and click **Page Number** and **Format Page Numbers**. Select **1, 2, 3** and **Start At**. Enter **3** and click **OK**. Now click **Page Number** and under "Bottom of Page," click the **position** you want. Arabic number **3** will appear in the footer.

To insert numbers on the *odd* and *even* pages in both of these sections, click your cursor in their **footers**, click **Page Number**, and under "Bottom of Page," click the **position** you want.

After you get past Section 5, and beginning with "First Page Footer, Section 6" (actual page 19), numbers should appear automatically in all First Page, Even Page, and Odd Page footers.

I highly recommend using drop folios instead of page numbers at the tops of your pages. Although you do have to unlink some of your footers, putting numbers in footers allows easy insertion of header text. I used drop folios in all the books I self-published except those concerning self-publishing, and I intend to use drop folios in all the books I publish in the future. I used header-placed numbers in this book just to show you how it looks when you follow the instructions for inserting header-placed numbers.

Deleting Page Numbers

To delete the header-placed page numbers in a section, click your cursor first on one of the even (or odd) pages (not in its header) in that section. (Double-click the page's text if the header box is in view.) Click the **Insert** tab and then click **Page Number** in the "Header and Footer" group. Click **Remove Page Numbers** in the box that comes up. All of the even (or odd) numbers *in that section* (and sometimes in other linked sections) will disappear. If the number was odd, all the odd numbers in that section will be deleted, but *only* the odd numbers. If the number was even, all the even numbers in that section will be deleted, but *only* the even numbers. You will have to delete the odd or even numbers remaining in other sections separately.

You can use the same procedure to remove footer-placed numbers that are on *odd* and *even* pages, but it *won't* remove them if they are in *First Page Footers*. To remove numbers that are in First Page Footers, you must use a different procedure. Click your cursor anywhere on the desired **First Page** and click the **Insert** tab. In the "Header and Footer" group, click **Footer** and then **Edit Footer** in the BUILT-IN dialog box. Your cursor will appear to the left of the drop folio. On your keyboard, click **Delete** *twice* and the number disappears. To use **Edit Footer** to remove folios from First Page Footers in other sections, click your cursor on the left side of each number and then double-click **Delete**. Or, highlight the number and click **Delete** once.

To remove *all* page numbers, you must do this in all remaining sections in which page numbers still appear.

Persisting to the End

Since you are now well armed with all necessary page-numbering skills, just continue to insert your own numbers to the end of your book block. Good luck! If you breeze through this task successfully, you will have completed one of the most daunting formatting procedures known to man. (Women, more than likely, will not have found merely numbering pages all that difficult.)

What to Do When All Else Fails

If you just can't get the numbering procedure to work for you, simply **Delete** the page-numbering template you are working on. Bring up your "4. Book Block with Section Breaks" and make another **Save As** template named "5. Book Block with Section Breaks Unlinked." Then unlink *all* headers and *all* footers in the entire book. Then reinsert your page numbers in each section. **Save** your work before continuing. Name it "6. Book Block with Page Numbers." When told that you already have a file by that name, click **yes** when asked if you want to replace it.

Chapter Seven

INSERTING TEXT INTO HEADERS

Most authors put the titles of their books in headers on verso (left, even-numbered) pages and the titles of their chapters (or other book elements) in headers on recto (right, odd-numbered) pages. Some insert their book titles on verso pages and their names on recto pages.

In each of these cases, most authors also insert their page numbers in headers. Other authors insert their page numbers in footers as drop folios. You can write whatever you like in either headers or footers, on whatever pages you want, once you understand the exact procedures required.

If you follow the most commonly used style guides, you will want some pages in your book to display no text and no page numbers in their headers. Generally, these pages include blank pages, parts of front matter, part pages, photos, illustrations, and *first* pages of chapters and other elements. The latter mentioned *first* pages are permitted drop folios but not header text.

This requirement brings up the question, How do you now insure that the same header text that appears on all the other pages in a section will not also appear on its first page?

To find out, bring up your "6. Book Block with Page Numbers" template. Make a **Save As** copy and name it "7. Book Block with Header Text."

Click *on* the **Show/Hide button** and scroll down to the *second* page of the *first* more-than-one-page section in which you want to insert header text. Click your cursor somewhere on that page. You are ready, at last, to insert your text into headers.

INSERTING HEADER TEXT

Because your First Page Header always remains without header text or page number, your first header text entry will be on the *second*, verso page in each section. (But not if you have a photo on that page and your text resumes on the next recto page.) Click your cursor anywhere on the first even, verso page of your "Contents" (actual page 8 on the chart).

Click the **Insert** tab. In the "Header & Footer" group, click **Header**. In the BUILT-IN dialog box that comes up, click **Edit Header** at the bottom of the box. Notice that the "Header & Footer Tools" and "Design" tabs come up active.

Your cursor appears inside the header box, on the *left* side of the page and on the *left* side of the even page number, which is now inside a little shaded box. Click your cursor on the **right** side of the number. The number's shaded box is now gone. Use your keyboard spacebar to move the cursor six spaces (or whatever distance you prefer) to separate the number from the header text you are about to insert. Then type in the **title** of your book (or whatever else you want). You might want to use *italics* to help distinguish your header text from your book's text.

You will now find that no header text appears on your First Page Header, but that the title of your book does appear in *all* the Even Page headers you have in this section.

To enter text in headers on odd, recto pages, click your cursor inside the header on the following Odd Page. This time, your cursor appears on the *right* side of the header box and immediately to the *left* of the odd number. Without spacing or doing anything else, begin typing in **Contents** (or whatever else you want). After you type the last letter in "Contents," hit your **spacebar** six times or more to space your header text away from the page number.

You will now find that "Contents" appears in *all* the Odd Page headers you might have in this section.

One other note: You can move a header's text to the left, center, or right position in the header by using the spacebar to insert more spaces between a page's number and its header text. But using the **Align Text** buttons in the "Home" tab's "Paragraph" group also moves the *page numbers* along with the header text. But, there is an easier way. When your page number is on the *left* side of *even* pages, you can reposition your header text as follows:

Assuming you have clicked **Insert/Header/Edit Header**, the "Header & Footer Tools" and "Design" tabs appear at about the center of the top menu bar. Click the **Design** tab if it is not active. Click your cursor immediately to the left of the first letter in your header text. In the "Position" group, click the little **icon** that reads **Insert Alignment Tab**. In the ALIGNMENT TAB dialog box that comes up, select the "Alignment" **position** you want. Leave everything else as it is and click **OK**. Your header text will move to your chosen position.

You can also do this *before* typing in your header text by using the above "Alignment" procedure to position your cursor in the *center* or on the *right* side of the page. Then type in your text.

This also works when your page number is odd and on the right side of the header, but you must click your cursor immediately on the *right* side of the *ending* letter in your header text. Then click the **Insert Alignment Tab icon** in the "Position" group. In the ALIGNMENT TAB dialog box that comes up, click **Center** and **OK**. Your header text moves to a little right of center in the header. To center it *exactly*, click your cursor on the *left* side of the page number and hit your **spacebar** repeatedly until the text is centered. This procedure will move an odd page's header text to the header's approximate center, but it *won't* move the text to the header's left side.

Continue inserting your header text in each following section. When you get down to the section where all following Even Page headers remain *linked* (Section 6), the Even Page text (usually your book's title) will repeat itself in every section remaining throughout the book. But you will have to insert your Odd Page text in the first Odd Page Header in each remaining section in the book (because they are all *unlinked* and you want *different* text in each section).

When you are finished with all your headers, be sure to **Save** your "7. Book Block with Header Text."

MINDING THE INSTRUCTIONS

If you have followed my instruction *exactly* as given previously concerning page setup, section breaks, and page numbers, you should have had little trouble inserting text into your headers. But if you can't seem to get it to come out right, just delete the template, make a new **Save As** "7. Book Block with Header Text" template from "6. Book Block with Page Numbers" and start over again.

As confusing and frustrating as all this sounds, you will eventually get the hang of it if you keep practicing these procedures. But be warned that weird, unexpected things can happen if you deviate too far from the instructions I have offered.

On the other hand, you might just discover much easier ways to accomplish these tasks.

Chapter Eight

EDITING & REVIEWING YOUR BOOK BLOCK

Congratulations! You have completed the formatting of your book block.

But wait! There's one other thing you should do before converting your book block file to PDF. Even though you are probably sick of reading and rereading your wonderful book, you should go over all of its pages at least one more time.

To help you do this, I offer the following list of suggestions:

1. If you imported a previously completed, double-spaced manuscript into your trim-sized page format, you had to reformat its line spacing and possibly its font use. One more time, you should go through your entire book block after this change to correct any spacing errors and misplaced headings. And, if you have not already done so, you must also change the page numbers in your table of contents to agree with your new setup. Even if you import a single-spaced manuscript, and you change its line spacing significantly, you might have to make similar minor corrections.

2. When you checked **Mirror Margins** on your PAGE SETUP dialog box, you enabled **Print Preview** to display all the pages in your book as multiple groups of two pages

each. Each group of two pages displays one even-numbered page joined to one odd-numbered page.

Using the panoramic view provided by **Print Preview** set at 10% **zoom**, you can easily see whether or not all pages required to appear on recto (right, odd-numbered) pages actually appear on those pages. For each of those recto-required pages that appear on verso (left, even-numbered) pages, you must insert a section break at the bottom of the page *preceding* that page and choose **Odd page** on the BREAK dialog box. (Be sure to unlink the header on that page.) Word will then insert a blank, even page between the ending odd page of the last chapter or other element and the next odd page on which the recto-required page is to appear.

Go through your entire book block and insert corrective **Odd page** section breaks where needed. Remember, the added pages will show up only on **Print Preview**, and no page number or header text will appear or can be written on them.

3. Go through your entire book block again—especially after you insert additional section breaks—and check each page for appropriate, sequential page numbers. Insure that all pages requiring invisible numbers have no visible ones.

4. Recheck all headers to see that verso and recto texts appear only on their respective pages and not at all on forbidden pages.

5. Check for consistency in spacing on first pages of all chapters and other elements. Are all chapter titles and

titles of other elements spaced down their pages an equal number of spaces? Do all texts begin an equal number of spaces beneath their titles? Are all paragraphs indented equally?

6. And finally, if you have the stomach for it, read your entire book again for errors in spelling and grammar. And while you are at it, why not imagine that you are a new, unbiased reader and try to gauge the book's overall impact on your senses and sensibilities. Have you left anything out that the reader should be told? Have you overloaded some chapters with inconsequential details? (I may be guilty of this in the book you are reading.)

Remember, if you choose to pursue self-publishing your book with any firm's "do-it-all-yourself" publishing program, your book block will be printed *exactly* as you submit it. (After your book has been made "Print Ready," you *can* click the **Change** button for any submission after proof-reading it and resubmit corrections and/or changes, but why put yourself through this.)

When you think your book block is exactly as you want it to be printed, make a **Save As** copy of your "7. Book Block with Header Text" and name it "8. Book Block, PDF Ready."

Chapter Nine

CREATING YOUR BOOK'S COVER

Some self-publishing firms, CreateSpace for example, provide their authors with a choice of book cover "templates" free of charge. All the work of formatting these templates to meet technical requirements and specifications has already been done. A prospective author can select one of the cover designs available on one of the trim sizes offered and insert on it his or her book's title, the author's name, and the back cover blurb. Or, he or she can use CreateSpace's pre-formatted, blank templates to create a custom-made cover.

However, in this book I will not cover the details of using such templates. I feel confident that any of you can explore and use this option on your own if you would rather avoid the technicalities of formatting your book's cover from scratch. But if you do use a pre-formatted template, you will miss out on the fun and satisfaction of doing it all yourself.

In this chapter, you will find every design and formatting detail necessary to construct your book's cover while using only Microsoft Word (and possibly Adobe Photoshop Elements if you use photos or artwork on your cover). But before beginning this task, I suggest that you read the cover specifications provided by whatever self-publishing firm you are choosing to go with. Don't let their instructions scare you. Follow my instructions carefully, and you will end up with a well-designed book cover that exactly meets virtually any firm's specifications.

FORMATTING YOUR BOOK'S COVER

My self-publishing firm, CreateSpace, prefers that my book's cover be created on a single 18" x 12" layout page. Other sizes of layout pages are acceptable, they say, provided that CreateSpace's specified dimensions for minimum margins, trim sizes, and bleed areas are observed. The cover—a one-piece construct consisting of front cover, spine, and back cover—must be centered horizontally and vertically on this layout page. If the publisher you choose specifies a different size layout page, center your cover on that size page and adapt my instructions accordingly.

Creating Your Cover's Page Layout Sheet

To create your page layout sheet, open a **New** Word document, check to see that Word's page view is set on **Print Layout**, and follow the instructions below:

Click the **Page Layout** tab. In the "Page Setup" group, click the little **arrow** down at its bottom, right corner. On the PAGE SETUP dialog box that comes up, click the **Paper** tab and enter the following:

Paper tab
  Paper size:
    Width: **18"**   Use the arrows to enter these width and
                          height numbers or type them in.
    Height: **12"**

Now click the **Margins** tab on the PAGE SETUP dialog box. On the "Orientation" section, select **Landscape**. You now have a single page that is 18" wide by 12" high on which to create your book's cover. But don't click OK yet. Before continuing with the next step, you must calculate the width of your book's spine.

Calculating Your Book's Spine Width

On the downloadable cover specifications file I mentioned above, CreateSpace gives its formula for calculating spine width. When your book is to be printed on "Standard White Paper," its spine width, in inches, will be equal to "Number of pages x .002252."

This formula should be acceptable to most publishers. To be sure, go to your self-publisher's website and look for a similar formula for determining spine width. Or, look for an interactive "spine width calculator."

You *must* calculate your book's spine width in order to continue designing your cover.

Since I don't know how many pages are in your book, I will enter figures below for a book with 176 pages. And I will explain how I got these figures so that you can enter figures based on your own book.

For a book with 176 pages, the spine width will be:

176 x .002252 = 0.3963 inches

Round off that result to 0.4 inches and you're all set. Now, go back to the "Margins" tab on the PAGE SETUP dialog box.

Calculating Page Setup Margins

For a book of 6" x 9" trim size, enter the numbers given below for your margins. I will explain below how to calculate all these margin dimensions.

Margins tab
Top:	**1.5"**	Enter this dimension here.
Bottom:	**1.5"**	Enter this dimension here.
Left:	**2.8"**	Enter your own calculations here.
Right:	**2.8"**	Enter your own calculations here.

The Top and Bottom margins, which will always be equal, are arrived at by subtracting the height of your book's trim size (9") from the height of the setup sheet (12") and dividing that number by 2.

The Left and Right margins, which also will always be equal, are calculated as shown below:

```
   6"    Front cover trim width
+ 0.4"   Spine width (Enter your own book's spine width.)
+ 6"     Back cover trim width
 12.4"   Total (Your total may differ.)
```

```
  18.0"   Width of setup sheet
 -12.4"   Total width of front cover, spine, and back cover.
   5.6"   Your result may differ.
```

5.6"/2 = **2.8"** Left and Right margins (for book with 0.4" spine width)

Leave all other options in the PAGE SETUP dialog box as is and click **OK**. A box will come up that says, "One or more margins are set outside the printable area of the page." Click the button labeled **Ignore**.

Formatting Cover Columns

So that you can see the full width of your cover's layout page, click on and move to the left the little slider at the bottom, right of your screen until your layout page just fills your screen. Or, click the **View** tab and then, in the "Zoom" group, click **Zoom**. In the ZOOM dialog box, under "Zoom to," click the "Percent" window **arrow** to **50%** or so. Click **OK** and your cover setup page now shrinks to just fill your screen horizontally. (You may have to choose a different percentile number if your screen is wider than mine.)

You must now divide the total width of your book's front cover, spine, and back cover into columns. Begin this by clicking the **Page Layout** tab. In the "Page Setup" group, click **Columns.** On the dropdown menu, click **More Columns** at the bottom of the box and enter the following:

COLUMNS dialog box:
  Number of Columns __2__   Click arrow to select.
  Width and spacing
   Col # Width Spacing
    1:      **6"**   **0.4"** Enter your own "Spacing"
                           (your book's spine width).

Check to see that **Equal column width** is checked, and then click **OK**.

When you look at the ruler above your document screen, you will note that your cover's setup page now appears in two columns of **6"** width, separated by a **0.4"** space.

Now go to the "Paragraph" group of the "Page Layout" tab. Under "Indent," enter **numbers** or click the **arrows** of the "Indent Left" and "Indent Right" windows to display **0.5"** in both windows. Leave everything else in the "Paragraph" group as is.

Apply the **Show/Hide** indicator and click your cursor on the top, left position in the *left* column. Press and hold down **Enter** on your keyboard until the left margin of both left and right columns are filled with the **Show/Hide** symbol. Leave a few spaces at the bottom of the right column or your cursor will jump down to another added page. (If it does, just press **Backspace** on your keyboard until the added page is gone.) Now click your cursor on the **bottom** of the *left* column.

On the "Page Layout tab," in the "Page Setup" group, click **Breaks.** On the PAGE BREAKS dialog box that drops down, click **Column.** A column break will appear at the bottom of the left column. To be sure the break is at the very bottom of the column, click your cursor immediately above it and press **Enter** on your keyboard. When the break disappears, press **Delete** to make it reappear at the bottom of the column.

Formatting the Spine

Your next step is that of formatting your book's spine. Click the **Insert** tab and go to the "Text" group. Click the **icon** labeled "Text Box." In the BUILT-IN dialog box that comes up, click **Draw Text Box** down at the bottom of the box. A large plus sign (+) will appear on the position your mouse pointer occupies.

Move that + sign, which now symbolizes your cursor, to a spot somewhere around the top, center of the left column and click your **mouse**. A small box appears. When you release your mouse button after inserting the box, a new tab appears at about the center of the top menu bar. It is labeled "Drawing Tools" with the word "Format" beneath. In the "Size" group, enter the following:

Shape Height: **9"**

Shape Width: **0.4"**   Enter or click arrow to show *your* book's spine width. Then press **Enter** on your keyboard.

You are now going to move your 9" x .4" text box to the horizontal and vertical center of your layout page. There are two ways to do this. The first way is easier, but I will also tell you the second way so you'll know what's involved in this.

For the first and easiest way, click your cursor anywhere inside the text box. Under the "Drawing Tools" and **"Format"** tabs, in the "Arrange" group, click the **Align icon**. On the menu that comes down, click **Align Center.** This will move your text box to the horizontal center of your layout page.

Next, in the "Arrange" group, click the **Align icon** again. On the dropdown menu, click **Align Middle**. This will center your text box vertically. Your text box should now be positioned *exactly* between your front and back covers.

For the second way to position your text box, click your cursor inside the text box. In the "Arrange" group, click **Position.** At the bottom of the box that drops down, click **More Layout Options**. On the LAYOUT dialog box that comes up, under the "Position" tab, enter the following:

Horizontal
   Absolute position   **8.8"** to the right of **Page** (Click arrow to select. *See note below.)
Vertical
   Absolute position   **1.5"** below **Page** (Click arrow to select. **See note below.)

Leave all else as is and click **OK.**

Notes:
   * This dimension equals the sum of your front cover's trim width (6") and the left *or* right margin set earlier on your page setup sheet (2.8").

   ** This dimension equals your cover's trim height (9") subtracted from the height of your page setup sheet (12"), which number is then divided by 2.

With your text box centered between your front and back covers, you are now ready to enter text into your book's spine. But first, the direction of the text has to be changed. If your cursor is not already there, click it anywhere inside the text box. The box will become outlined in dashes.

Then, beneath the "Drawing Tools" tab, click the **Format** tab if it is not already active. In the "Text" group, click the little **icon** that reads "Text Direction." On the dropdown menu, click **Rotate all text 90°**. You are now ready to enter text into your book's spine.

Should you ever wish to go back to change formatting in your text box, click your cursor anywhere inside the spine. This causes the spine to become outlined in dashes and brings up the "Drawing Tools" and "Format" tabs and menu bar. Click the **Format** tab beneath the "Drawing Tools" tab if it is not already active.

Inserting Text into the Spine

This is the really fun part! To help you see everything in more detail, adjust the **slider** at the bottom, right of your screen to enlarge your text box to 150% or more. Now manipulate your screen's horizontal and vertical bars to center the spine and display its top half. With your mouse clicked at the very top of the text box spine, hit your keyboard's **spacebar** several times to lower your cursor an inch or so from the top of the spine.

Now to set the "Internal margins" of your book's spine. In the "Shape Styles" group, click the little **arrow** at the bottom, right corner of the box. The FORMAT SHAPE dialog box comes up. From the list of options on the left side of the box, click the words **Text Box** to bring up its options on the right side of the box.

Under "Internal margin," enter **0.05** into both the "Right" and "Left" windows. Then **Close** the FORMAT SHAPE dialog box.

Click the **Home** tab, choose a **font** (serif, sans serif, bold, or whatever you like) and select a **font size** that is as large as you can fit into the spine's width and still have room to type in your complete *main* title, followed by an appropriate space and then your name. Before typing the title, you may wish to set your keyboard for all capital letters. Also, select a **font color** for your text from the "Font" group if you wish. Now type in your book's title, several spaces, and your name.

If the font size you choose is too large, the text will become clipped when it intrudes into the text box's margins you previously set. If this happens, back off your font size one size at a time until you get the maximum useable size.

If the font size is ok, but you don't have enough room to type in your title and your name, **Delete** some of the spaces preceding and following your title and some of the spaces between your title and your name. If there still is not enough room, you will have to reduce your font size.

If your book's title is not centered exactly between the vertical sides of the text box, do this:

With your cursor clicked inside the spine's text box, click **Format** under the "Drawing Tools" tab on the top menu bar. Then click the little **arrow** at the bottom, right corner of the "Shape Styles" group. The FORMAT SHAPE dialog box comes up. From the list of options on the left side of the box, click the words **Text Box** to bring up its options on the right side of the box.

Under "Internal margin," click the **down arrow** of the "Right" box until its reading is **0**". Your spine's text should now be almost against the spine's right side. Then enter the decimal number **0.08** into the box. If this number does not center the spine's text between the sides of its text box, enter lesser or greater numbers until you get it centered. Obviously, if your book has a thick spine, you will have to enter much greater numbers. Just keep experimenting with different numbers until you get the text centered, and then click **Close** at the bottom, right corner of the dialog box.

Now to remove the border lines around your text box, in the "Shape Styles" group, click the words **Shape Outline**, not the icon. Then on the dropdown menu, click **No Outline**. Now click your cursor anywhere outside the text box.

This action removes the lines surrounding your book's spine. Since you can no longer see the spine's outline unless you click on the spine, you may want to wait until you are through with the front and back covers before you remove the lines. But be sure that you do remove them, because they will print if you leave them there.

If you want a colored cover, click your cursor *outside* the spine's text box and then click the **Page Layout** tab. In the "Page Background" group, click **Page Color.** On the dropdown menu, position your cursor over the **color** you want and click it. Your entire 18" x 12" cover page (except for the spine) will fill with the color you selected, but that's OK. This "bleed" will be trimmed off.

To fill the spine with the cover's color, click inside the spine and then click **Format** under the "Drawing Tools" tab if it is not already active. In the "Shape Styles" group, click the words **Shape Fill**, not the icon. Click the **color** of your cover and the spine will fill with that color. If you want the spine a *different* color, click the color of your choice.

However, I do not recommend coloring your book's spine with a color that differs from that of your front and back covers. Your publishing firm's printer cannot guarantee that a book's spine width will always be positioned so as to break exactly between the front and back covers. If this doesn't matter to you, and you still want a different colored spine, go ahead. You may hear from your publisher about this, but he will accept it if you insist.

Although you are not yet finished with your book's cover, **Save** your work at this point so that you can return to this save point if you need to. Name it "Cover, Spine."

INSERTING TEXT & IMAGES ON YOUR COVER

Your front and back covers need not be overly ornate or complex in design. Personally, I believe that a clean, simply designed cover is more likely to attract attention than one that is filled from edge to edge with multiple, flamboyant colors that often render almost unreadable the text on top of them.

Your Front Cover

Reduce your cover's size to about 60%, using the slider at the bottom of your screen. Click the **Home** tab, click *on* the **Show/Hide** button in the "Paragraph" group, and then click your cursor in the right column (front cover) about three or four lines down. Note the little arrows on the ruler bar at the top of your screen. They denote your left and right margins.

In the "Home" tab's "Paragraph" group, **center** your cursor at a pleasing vertical position and enter your **main title** (and **subtitle**, if you want and have room), followed by several vertical spaces and your **name**. Or, put your name toward the bottom of the page if you like. For all the text on your *front* cover, you may wish to use a sans serif font. But choose a serif font if you like. I used Georgia, a serif font, on this book.

For your main title, use the largest font size that you can fit appropriately between the cover's right and left margins without going outside them. If your book has a lengthy main title, you may have to break it up into several lines in order to use a font of significant size. Use a **bold** font if you like, as well as your choice of **colors** for the letters.

Using the procedure I outlined earlier in the chapter on "Preparing and Inserting Images," insert whatever **photo**, **artwork**, or other type of **image** you wish to display on your cover. If you do use an image or images, choose colorful ones if possible, but keep them simple. (They will retain their own colors and background if inserted on a colored cover.)

My wife, Alma, drew the images for three of my book covers. If you want to see them, go to amazon.com, enter my name in the search box, and, on the page that comes up, click on *Bible Prophecy in a Nutshell* to see her drawing of angels with trumpets. Click on *Strawberry Lane* and *Return to Strawberry Lane* to see their cover images.

Position your image in whatever area you think best enhances your front cover. Insert appropriate **vertical spaces** between all textual elements and images to give your cover a balanced, well-crafted appearance.

Inserting text and images on your front or back cover will push down the bottom lines on the cover (front or back) you are working on. This causes a second page to appear beneath your cover page. **Delete** these added spaces (and the extra page) as follows:

If you are working on the *back* cover, click your cursor on the *bottom* line of that cover. Then click **Delete** repeatedly until the *Column break* reappears on that bottom line. If you are working on the *front* cover, click your cursor on the *bottom* line of that cover and click **Delete** repeatedly until the extra page disappears.

Your Back Cover

Click *on* the **Show/Hide** button and then click your cursor in the left column (back cover). Again, note the little arrows on the ruler bar at the top of your screen. They denote your left and right margins. Compose the text for your back cover just as if you were writing it all on a separate sheet of paper.

On a line or two down from the top of your back cover, type in a centered, large-font **text line** that will act as a "hook" for your potential reader. Use a question or a startling statement to arouse curiosity. Follow up the hook with a short summary of what the book is about and what it offers to do for its readers. Look at the back covers of other books, especially those that are similar to yours, to see how those authors did it.

Beyond this advice, I refer you to Dan Poynter's all-time classic book, *Self-Publishing Manual: How to Write, Print and Sell Your Own Book.* On page 51 of the Fifteenth Edition of this book, Poynter offers a detailed tutorial on "Drafting Your Back-Cover Sales Copy." In later editions of his book, instructions concerning back cover copy may, of course, begin on a different page.

Your ISBN and Bar Code

Be sure to leave room on your back cover for your bar code at the bottom, right corner. (More about this later.) To create or buy a bar code, however, you must first obtain an ISBN (International Standard Book Number) for your book.

Obtaining Your ISBN

You will need a "Bookland EAN/13 with add on" ISBN. This number will contain all the information necessary to identify the publisher of your book, its title, price, and other related data. Your bar code will incorporate this ISBN in its construction.

Some self-publishing firms (CreateSpace, for example) offer to provide their authors with an ISBN free of charge for each book published with them. Or, they will permit you to purchase your own ISBN. If your publisher supplies your ISBN, that firm technically becomes the publisher of your book. If *you* supply your own ISBN, *you* become the publisher.

If you choose to buy your ISBN, you will have to buy a block of 10—the minimum number you can buy—for $275 (as of the date of this writing). You can obtain them from Bowker Bar Code Service at www.bowker.com.

Even without considering the cost of buying my own ISBNs, I have no interest in starting my own publishing business; I just want to get my books into print and on Amazon for sale. You may have different goals in mind. If so, buy your own ISBNs and tell your self-publishing firm that you are doing so. You will then report your ISBN's numbers to them when you sign up with them to publish your book.

Obtaining & Inserting Your Bar Code

Some self-publishing firms (CreateSpace, for example) will provide and install a bar code on your book's back cover free of charge. Should you choose a firm that requires *you* to obtain and install a bar code, I offer the instructions below.

When publishing my first book with BookSurge, I accessed a link on their website that led to a site on which authors could construct their bar codes free of charge. But that site repeatedly warned prospective bar code creators that there was no guarantee that the finished product would always scan acceptably. Rather than risk this uncertainty and spend the time creating my own bar code, I opted to purchase one ready-made from Bar Code Graphics at 1-800-662-0701 for the paltry sum of $15. You can also go to their website, www.createbarcodes.com, and get one.

To get your barcode from these nice people, you first have to register with them, give a password, and provide a credit card number. You will then get an e-mail confirming your account with them. To place your order, you must give them your ISBN and your book's price. Then you will receive your bar code via an e-mail attachment. It will come as an Encapsulated PostScript (EPS) file. **Save** this EPS file before continuing with the instructions below.

These instructions are for inserting a bar code on a *white* cover. Be sure to read the next page before beginning to insert your bar code on a *colored* cover. When you are ready to insert your bar code, bring up your book's cover file and click your cursor in the left column, the back cover. Click *on* the **Show/Hide** button. Using the vertical ruler to the left side of your back cover, click your cursor on the left margin at about **1 ½** inches from the bottom. This will put your cursor at the top, left corner of the spot your bar code will occupy temporarily. Now, click **Insert/Picture.** On the INSERT PICTURE dialog box that comes up, navigate to the EPS barcode you saved and click on it. Then click **Insert.** Your bar code will appear on the bottom, left side of your page.

If your back cover's line spacing is set to anything more than **single space**, only a narrow strip of your bar code may appear. If this happens, you must first reset to **single space** your line spacing for the *single* line your cursor is clicked on.

If the barcode is larger than you want, you can downsize it slightly by clicking on it, clicking **Format** under the "Picture Tools" tab, and reducing its **width** in the "Size" group to a *maximum* of 2.0 inches. If the width is at or below 2.0 inches, leave it as it is.

You can reposition your bar code horizontally by clicking on it and then clicking the **Align Right** button in the **Home** tab's "Paragraph" group. Your bar code should now relocate to the *right* margin of your left column. If you would rather put your bar code in a different *vertical* location, click on it and press **Delete** on your keyboard. Now, in the left margin, click your cursor on the vertical location you want before you reinsert your bar code. Then **reinsert** it and click the **Align Right** button to reposition it horizontally.

Alternately, you can reposition your bar code as follows: click on the bar code and then click **Format** under the "Picture Tools" tab. In the "Arrange" group, click **Wrap Text.** On the dropdown menu, click **In Front of Text**. Now you can click on and drag your bar code to where you want it.

The instructions you have just read assume that the back cover of your book will be white. If you want to color your cover, you will have to install a **Text Box** of sufficient size in which to insert your bar code. A bar code inserted on top of a color may not scan correctly.

To insert a text box, click your cursor somewhere at the bottom of your back cover. Then click the **Insert** tab. In the "Text" group, click **Text box.** At the bottom of the BUILT-IN dialog box that comes up, click **Draw Text Box.** Your cursor will appear as a large "+" sign. Position it about 1/8" above where you want your barcode's top, left corner to appear. Then click your **mouse button**. When you release your mouse button, a rectangle of white appears, surrounded by your cover's color. Now, in the "Size" group at the right end of the "Format" tool bar, enter **1.25**" in the "Shape Height" box and **2.25"** in the "Shape Width" box. Press **Enter** on your keyboard and the text box adjusts to that size.

If you don't like the position your text box is in, click **Undo** several times until it disappears. Then reinsert it in a different location.

Alternately, if you want to tackle the math, you can re-position your text box as follows:

Click your cursor inside the text box. Click **Format** beneath the "Drawing Tools" tab. Then click **Position** in the "Arrange" group. On the menu that comes up, click **More Layout Options.** In the LAYOUT dialog box that comes up, click the **Position** tab. Now enter the horizontal and vertical dimensions that will place your text box where you want it. These dimensions for this book are:

"Horizontal"
    Absolute position **3.25"** to the right of **Column**

"Vertical"
    Absolute position **8.5"** below **Top Margin**
                Leave everything else as is and click **OK.**

Adjust these figures to position your own text box where you want it. You can see that it is much easier, however, just to **Undo** your insertion and try a new position.

After you get your bar code's text box correctly positioned, you should delete the border around it. You must do this *before* you insert your bar code in it. Remove the text box's border as follows:

Click your cursor inside the text box. Click **Format** beneath the "Drawing Tools" tab. In the "Shape Styles" group, click **Shape Outline**. Then on the dropdown menu, click **No Outline.** The border around the text box disappears.

Now to insert your bar code in the text box, click your cursor inside the text box at the top, left corner. Set that line to single space and insert your barcode as instructed above for a white cover. It will appear inside the text box on a white background. To center the bar code vertically inside the text box, click on it, then click the **Page Layout** tab. In the "Paragraph" group, under "Spacing," enter **2 pt** or **3pt** or **4 pt** in the "Spacing Before" box and then press **Enter** on your keyboard. Click **Undo** to try a different spacing number.

A bar code inserted *in a text box* does *not* add line spaces below, but a bar code inserted alone (*not* in a text box) causes everything beneath it to move *down* about four spaces. In the latter case, you will have to **Delete** those spaces. Recheck the front cover to see that everything is OK. Click **Save**.

All of this concerning obtaining and inserting a bar code can be avoided, however, if you self-publish your book with Createspace. As I said at the beginning of this chapter, Createspace will not only provide a bar code, but they will install it on your book's back cover free of charge.

Chapter Ten

CONVERTING YOUR WORD FILES TO PDF WITH ADOBE ACROBAT

There are many ways to convert a Microsoft Word file to PDF. Some self-publishing firms prefer that you use Adobe Acrobat to do it, but they *will* accept files converted by other less expensive programs. I asked my Publishing Consultant at CreateSpace if they accept files converted to PDF by conversion programs other than Adobe Acrobat, and she said, "Yes."

NON-ADOBE PDF CONVERSION PROGRAMS

As of this writing, you can download a free PDF Writer from *cutepdf.com*. They also offer a professional version for $49. A free suite of office programs at *openoffice.org* also includes a PDF converter. Or, you can buy one of the less expensive PDF conversion programs available in office supply and electronics stores, but you're on your own with all of these. I've used only Adobe Acrobat, so I can't advise you on the other PDF programs. They will probably do a quality conversion that your self-publishing firm will accept.

However, some non-Adobe PDF conversion programs may offer you limited control over the conversion process. For example, they may not be able to convert your book cover's colors to CMYK: cadmium, magenta, yellow, and black. (Although CreateSpace *does* accept RGB colors.)

And, non-Adobe software may not have a function similar to Acrobat's "Preflight," whereby you can test your converted PDF files to see that they turned out as you intended them to.

WORD'S ADOBE ACROBAT PDF CONVERTER

(This section applies to Word users who *do not* have Adobe Acrobat installed on their computers.)

Word's Free Adobe Acrobat PDF Converter

If you have Microsoft Word 2010 on your computer, this version of Word offers "free" Adobe Acrobat PDF conversion of your Word documents. "Free", that is, of charges above the amount you paid for Word 2010.

Word 2007 also offers Adobe Acrobat PDF conversion capabilities, but you have to download and install a free Word "add-in" program. With Word 2010, you don't have to download this "add-in." Word 2010 comes ready to convert files to PDF.

You can access the PDF conversion that Word 2010 provides as follows: **Open** the Word file you want to convert to PDF. Click **File** at the top, left of your screen. On the menu that drops down, click **Save As**.

The **Save As** dialog box that comes up should list the file you just opened. (If not, navigate to it from "documents" or "libraries" on the left side of the box.)

Enter your file's **name** in the "File Name" window of the SAVE AS dialog box. Click the **arrow** for the "Save as type" window and then click **PDF** on the drop-down menu. Put a check in the "Open file after publishing" box and see that the "Optimize for: Standard (publishing online and printing)" option has been selected.

Click **Save** and your file will be converted to PDF and displayed on top of your original Word file. But if the PDF file does not come up automatically, **Close** the Word file, navigate to the folder containing that Word file, and **open** the folder. Right click on the **PDF file** listed there and select **Open with Adobe Reader X** (or with whatever version of Adobe Reader you have). Your PDF file appears.

Limitations of Word's PDF Converter

Although using Word's PDF converter gives you a limited Adobe Acrobat conversion, the only control you have over its quality is the aforementioned "Optimize for: Standard (publishing online and printing)". You are not given options such as "Object level compression" on or off," "Convert colors to CMYK," "Embed all fonts," etc.

And, without Adobe Acrobat software actually installed on your computer, Word's PDF conversion gives you no "Preflight" with which to check and adjust your converted file. But Word does provide "Preflight" if you have a full version of Adobe Acrobat available on your computer. But if that is the case, why use Word's PDF converter instead of Adobe Acrobat's? Even so, Word's stand-alone converter may just give you a PDF file that your self-publisher will accept. Try it, if you like, and see.

ADOBE ACROBAT'S FREE TRIAL OFFER

Before you rush out and buy your own copy of Adobe Acrobat to convert your book and cover to PDF, you can download a free trial copy of Adobe Acrobat's latest version that is good for converting up to five documents. Go to **www.adobe.com**. On the page that comes up, position your cursor over **Download**. On the menu beneath it, click **Product trials.** On the page that comes up, under the heading "Downloads," position your cursor over **Adobe Acrobat XI Pro** or whatever version is available at the time you need it. On the options that appear beneath "Adobe Acrobat XI Pro," click **Try**. This will take you to a page labeled "Download a free trial of Acrobat XI." Then click **Download now**. (These instructions may change.)

Or, you may find it easier just to type into your browser **www.adobe.com/products/acrobatpro/tryout.html? promoid=DTELN** for a direct link to the trial download page.

As expensive as it is, you will probably not want to buy Adobe Acrobat if you know you are going to publish only one book. Otherwise, you might want to do as I did, bite the bullet and buy your very own copy of Adobe Acrobat's latest version.

USING ADOBE ACROBAT

If you use Adobe Acrobat, as I did, there are several ways to convert a file to PDF. You can open your Adobe Acrobat program and click **Create PDF,** you can click the **Acrobat** tab on Word's top menu bar, or you can use the **Adobe PDF**

Print command, which Adobe adds to programs that offer a **Print** function. I am going to tell you how to convert *your* files by using the **Adobe PDF Print** command. (If you are using a program other than Adobe Acrobat, follow that program's instructions.)

The instructions below are for the use of Adobe Acrobat Pro X (that is, version 10). If you are using an earlier version, my instructions will generally apply to its use, but there are small differences. On its website, CreateSpace offers skimpy instructions for the use of all versions of Adobe Acrobat.

To print these instructions, go to createspace.com and type **Creating a PDF** into the search box at the top, right corner of the screen. Press **Enter** on your keyboard. On the "Creating a PDF" page that comes up, click the selection that is titled in blue letters, **Creating a PDF**. The document that comes up has PDF instructions for all Acrobat versions available as of this writing.

USING THE ADOBE PDF PRINT COMMAND

Bring up and open your completed "8. Book Block, PDF Ready" file. Click **File** at the top, left corner of your screen and then click **Print** on the menu that drops down. In the PRINT dialog box that appears, proceed as follows:

Printer
    Adobe PDF   Click the arrow at the end of the window and select this.
    Printer Properties   Click this beneath the right end of the "Printer" widow.

SELECTING YOUR PDF DEFAULT SETTINGS

On the ADOBE PDF DOCUMENT PROPERTIES dialog box that comes up, click the **Adobe PDF Settings** tab if it is not already selected. To the right of "Default Settings," click the **arrow** at the end of the window and select **Press Quality** from the list that drops down. "Press Quality" will appear in the "Default Settings" window. Now click **Edit** to the right of the window. After a short delay, the PRESS QUALITY— ADOBE PDF SETTINGS dialog box comes up.

EDITING YOUR PRESS QUALITY SETTINGS

At the top, left corner of the above-named dialog box, under the heading "Press Quality," you will see in a vertical column six file folder icons that I will call "tabs." Each tab is labeled with a different settings function. The settings tab that first appears after the PRESS QUALITY—ADOBE PDF SETTINGS dialog box comes up is that of the "General tab."

The "General" Tab
Beneath "File Options," a window labeled "Compatibility" will contain **Acrobat 5.0 (PDF 1.4)**. If this does not appear in the window, click its **arrow** and select it from the list.

For the "Object Level Compression" window, click the **arrow** and select **Off.**

For the "Auto-Rotate Pages" window, select **Off.**

Leave all other settings in this dialog box as they are and click **Images**, the second settings tab at the top, left of the dialog box.

The "Images" Tab

There are three categories of images listed in this dialog box. Make changes only as specified in **bold** numbers and words, and leave all other settings as they are.

Color Images

Downsample: Bicubic Downsampling to   **305**   pixels per inch

for images above: **320**   pixels per inch

Compression: **JPEG**   Click the **arrow** and select this

Image Quality: **Maximum**   Select this

Grayscale Images

Downsample: Bicubic Downsampling to   **305**   pixels per inch

for images above: **320**   pixels per inch

Compression: **JPEG**   Click the **arrow** and select this

Image Quality: **Maximum**   Select this

Monochrome Images

Leave all settings as they are and click the **Fonts** tab at the top, left of the dialog box.

The "Fonts" Tab

Embed all fonts: Check to see that this is **selected** (has a checkmark in its box).

Subset embedded fonts: **Deselect** this. (Click off the checkmark in its box.)

When embedding fails: Check to see that **Cancel job** appears in this window. If not, click the **arrow** and **select** it.

Leave all other settings as they are and click the **Color** tab at the top, left of the dialog box.

The "Color" Tab

Under "Color Management Policies," click the **arrow** at the end of the window and select **Leave Color Unchanged** if you are converting your *book block* to PDF. If you are converting your book *cover*, select **Convert All Colors to CMYK**. (If you are using Adobe Acrobat *Standard* version or any other program that cannot convert colors to CMYK, you will not, of course, be offered this option. In that case, you should select **Leave Color Unchanged**.) As I said earlier, CreateSpace accepts RGB colors for your book's cover.

Leave the "Advanced Tab," and the "Standards Tab" as they are and click **Save As** at the bottom of the dialog box.

The SAVE ADOBE PDF SETTINGS AS dialog box comes up. Acrobat specifies the location at which your settings are saved, but you must assign a name to them:

File name: **Press Quality, Book Block**
Type this in the window if you are converting your *book block* to PDF.

Press Quality, Book Cover
Type this in the window if you are converting your book *cover* to PDF.

Save as type: **Adobe PDF Settings Files**   Check to see that this appears in the "Save as" window. If not, click the window's **arrow** and select it.

Now click **Save**. This will bring up the dialog box labeled PRESS QUALITY, BOOK BLOCK-ADOBE PDF SETTINGS or whatever name you gave your file.

Click **OK**. This will take you back to:

ADOBE PDF DOCUMENT PROPERTIES dialog box

In this dialog box, under the **Adobe PDF Settings** tab, you should see your settings title, "Press Quality, Book Block" or "Press Quality, Book Cover" in the "Default Settings" window.

In the future, whenever you convert any book to PDF, you won't have to go through all the **Edit** procedures to set up these specifications. When you get to "Default Settings" in the conversion process, just click the **arrow** and select **Press Quality, Book Block**, or **Press Quality, Book Cover** from those options listed. Then continue by following the instructions below.

COMPLETING YOUR PDF CONVERSION

Returning to the ADOBE PDF DOCUMENT PROPERTIES dialog box, proceed as follows:

Adobe PDF Settings tab

Adobe PDF Security: **None**   Check to see that this window contains the word "None." If not, click the **arrow** and select it.

Adobe PDF Page Size: Click the **arrow** to the right of the window and follow the instructions below:

If this is your first time to access "Page Size," its list may not include a useable size for your book block (**6 x 9**, for example), nor will it offer an **18 x 12** page size for your book cover's setup sheet. For that size and any other book block size not shown, you'll have to click **Add** to right of the window and continue with the ADD CUSTOM PAPER SIZE dialog box as depicted on the next page.

For future books, once you have added your trim sizes to the Paper Size list, click the Page Size **arrow**, select your trim page size, and then jump around the dash-enclosed section on the next page and continue at "Rely on systems fonts only" (directly beneath the dash-enclosed section).

ADD CUSTOM PAPER SIZE dialog box

Paper Names: **18 x 12**   Enter this or whatever name you want that is not already on the dropdown list above.

Paper size:

Width   **18**   Enter this or whatever width you want that is not listed above.

Height   **12**   Enter this or whatever height you want. Now, click **Add/Modify** at the bottom of the box. This will take you back to:

ADOBE PDF DOCUMENT PROPERTIES dialog box

Adobe PDF Page Size: Click the **arrow** for the "Page Size" window and select the **18 x 12** or other size you just entered.

"Rely on system fonts only"   **Deselect** this statement. (Click *off* the checkmark in its box.)

Now, on the ADOBE PDF DOCUMENT PROPERTIES dialog box, click the **Layout** tab. Under "Orientation," select **Portrait** for your *book block* or **Landscape** for your book *cover* and then click **OK** at the bottom of the box.

Clicking **OK** on the ADOBE PDF DOCUMENT PROPERTIES dialog box takes you back to the "Print" option of the "FILE" menu. Click the **Print box** (not "Save As" on the File menu). The SAVE PDF FILE AS dialog box appears as a flashing icon in the task bar at the bottom of your screen. Click that **icon** to bring up the dialog box. Proceed as follows:

SAVE PDF FILE AS dialog box

(Save location): Enter in the address window the place you want your PDF file saved.

File name: Enter **PDF Book Block** or **PDF Book Cover** or whatever name you prefer for the file you are converting. (If you are self-publishing with CreateSpace, you must precede the names of your files with your book's ISBN number.)

Save as type: This window should contain the words "PDF files."

Click **Save** and your file will be converted to PDF. The PDF file appears as a flashing icon in the task bar at the bottom of your screen. Click that **icon** to bring up the PDF.

On the PDF, you will have to click the **minus** button of the "Zoom Out" option on the upper menu bar to reduce the PDF's size.

TESTING YOUR PDF FILES IN ACROBAT'S PREFLIGHT

Before going on, let's verify what we have done. On the right side of the PDF document you are now looking at, click **Tools** and proceed as follows:

Tools   Click this.
  Print Production Click if no menu appears beneath it.
    Preflight   Click this in list under "Print Production".
      PREFLIGHT dialog box, "Profiles" tab
        "PDF analysis"   Click the **arrow** to left of this.

Pull the side bar down, if necessary, until you can select **List page objects, grouped by type of object**. Then click **Analyze** at the bottom, right side of the box.

The "Results" tab will become active. If you have images in your interior file or on your book's cover, click the "+" sign to the left of "Resolution of color and grayscale images is greater than 250 ppi." A list of pages on which you have images will appear. On the each of these pages, the color mode ("Gray scale" or "Color" as "RGB" or "CMYK") of the image will precede the image's resolution. The resolution of each image should read a minimum of "300.0 ppi" (although "299.0 ppi" is acceptable). Double-click each image or click the **Show** button to the right of each image listed if you want to see the images. (Drag the PREFLIGHT box to the side.) When you are finished looking at the images, click the "+" sign to the left of "Resolution . . ." to collapse the list of pages.

Now click the "+" sign to the left of "Overview." On the list that drops down, click the "+" sign to the left of "Fonts."

Beneath "Fonts" you will see "True Type font: Georgia" or whatever font or fonts you embedded in your PDF file.

In your book block, if you previously converted your images to *grayscale* using Photoshop, inserted them into your Word file, and then converted your Word file to PDF using Acrobat, you will find that your *grayscale* images are listed as "Color images" that are in RGB color mode when you check them in "Preflight." This is because Word arbitrarily changed your images back to RGB mode when you inserted them into your file. But not to worry, even though they are listed as being in Color-RGB mode, they will be in *grayscale* if you converted them to *grayscale* before you inserted them into your Word file. And, CreateSpace will accept your *grayscale* images even though they are listed as being in RGB color mode.

Even so, if you would rather have your book block's PDF images show up in "Preflight" as being in *grayscale* color mode, just follow the instructions below to reconvert them from RGB to *grayscale* using Acrobat's "Preflight" to do it.

Use the same above procedures to test your PDF cover file. Note that any color images inserted on your cover will appear in "Preflight" as being "Color images" in RGB or CMYK color mode. CreateSpace will accept either mode for color images.

To correct anything wrong, you will have to go back to your Word file, make corrections, and reconvert it to PDF.

HOW TO CONVERT YOUR PHOTOS TO GRAYSCALE IN YOUR PDF DOCUMENT

1. **Open** your PDF file.
2. Click **Tools** at the top, right side of the screen.

3. On the menu that drops down, click **Print Production** if a menu doesn't appear beneath it.
4. On the menu beneath "Print Production," click **Preflight**.
5. In the PREFLIGHT dialog box, under the "Profiles" tab, click the **arrow** to the left of "PDF fixups." (If necessary, pull the slide bar down to find this.)
6. On the list of options that drops down, click **Convert to grayscale**.
7. Click **Edit** on the right end of the blue "Convert to grayscale" bar.
8. On the left side of the PREFLIGHT: EDIT PROFILE dialog box that comes up, you will see a list of options beneath "Convert" in a blue bar. From that list, select **Images**.
9. Click **OK** at the bottom of the screen.
10. Back on the PREFLIGHT dialog box, at the bottom of the box, click **Analyze and fix**.
11. On the SAVE PDF FILE box that comes up, click **Save**. When asked if you want to replace the file, click **Yes**.
12. Back on the PREFLIGHT dialog box, click the **Profiles** tab.
13. Under "PDF analysis," (click arrow for options list), click **List page objects, grouped by type of object**.
14. At the bottom of the box, click **Analyze**.
15. On the PREFLIGHT dialog box, under the "Results" tab, click the "+" **sign** to the left of "Resolution of color and grayscale images."

Beneath the above, see that your images have been converted to Grayscale color mode.

To correct any failures that do not match the above results, you will have to go back to your Word file, correct whatever is wrong, and reconvert your Word file to PDF.

If "Preflight" proves your file is OK, it is now ready for upload to your self-publishing firm.

Chapter Eleven

CHOOSING YOUR PUBLISHER AND SUBMITTING YOUR PDF FILES

The procedures for submitting and uploading your PDF files will vary, of course, with the self-publishing firm you choose. Even so, I'll give you a few typical pointers that will more than likely apply to any firm you select. But first, you must choose a firm to go with.

CHOOSING YOUR SELF-PUBLISHING FIRM

When choosing a self-publishing firm, you will find yourself asking, "What specific services and qualities am I looking for, and how can I measure and compare the performance of each firm with all the others?"

Profiling the Firms

For those of you that have not already chosen a publisher for your book, I highly recommend that you buy Stacie Vander Pol's book, *Top Self Publishing Firms: How Writers Get Published, Sell More Books, and Rise to the top.* In chapter 1, Stacie says, "This book profiles the top twenty-six self-publishing firms based on their sales results."

The profile for each of these 26 firms details the firm's offerings and performance in the following categories:

Contact Info
Best Publishing Package
Additional Services
Trade Discounts
Royalties
Book Pricing
Author Purchases
Author Rights and Contract
Strengths
Weaknesses
Summary

At the top of each profile, Stacie summarizes her findings in a boxed "SNAPSHOP" that includes five evaluators of the firm's performance:

Sales Results
Amazon Royalties
Bookstore Royalties
Distribution
Overall Value

For each firm profiled, Stacie gives each of these evaluators a grade of Excellent, Very Good, Good, Okay, Above Average, Average, Below Average, Poor, or None. (If you buy her book, notice that Stacie chose CreateSpace to publish it.)

The book also contains other information about self-publishing that I'm sure you will find valuable.

Establishing Your Account

Before you can begin any serious efforts to start your self-publishing process, you must, obviously, establish an account with the firm of your choice. There is nothing difficult about doing this; just go to the firm's website and click on the link that says something like "Establish a new account." Follow the links and instructions on the pages that come up. If such links are not readily apparent, click on "Contact us," type in your desire to establish a new account, and wait for a reply.

SUBMITTING YOUR FILES TO CREATESPACE (AN EXAMPLE)

Before commenting on submitting and uploading your PDF files to CreateSpace, I must make a few preliminary remarks. I do not intend, in this book, to explain every step and detail of CreateSpace's publishing processes as I did for BookSurge in one of my previous self-publishing books, *How to Self-Publish Your Book with BookSurge for Less$$$*. Because such processes are subject to changes—changes that would require the correction and republishing of my book—I am going to stick to my primary goal, that of teaching you how to design and format your book using only Microsoft Word 2010. I'm confident that you can find your way around CreateSpace's website on your own.

Should you decide to go with CreateSpace, I'm going to make it easy for you. My CreateSpace Publishing Consultant is Whitney Strachan. You can reach her by phone or e-mail as follows:

Toll free: 877-814-3488 ext. 8149
Direct: (843) 760-8149
Email: wstracha@createspace.com.

(You might want to tell her that I suggested you contact her.)

I can assure you that Whitney does an outstanding job. She will answer your questions and help you set up an account in no time.

Among requests for information, you will be asked for a password and a valid credit card number that will be kept in CreateSpace's secure file. This card number can be used should you decide to purchase any of CreateSpace's helpful services or to buy your published books at a ridiculously low cost.

Once you open an account with CreateSpace, you will be assigned a "Member ID" and be given access to your own account page called your "Member Dashboard." From this page, you can access virtually everything that has to do with self-publishing your book.

To get your publication process started, you can choose from two basic options. These options are what I will call the "No-cost, unsupported PDF option" and the "Modest-cost, supported PDF option."

If you have confidence in your formatting expertise, you may wish to consider the "No-cost" option. However, for self-publishing your first book, I strongly advise you to choose the "Modest-cost" option. After publishing your first book this way, you will know what to expect should you choose the "No cost," free-of-charge option to publish your next book.

CreateSpace's No-Cost, Unsupported PDF Option

You *can* submit and upload your PDF files to CreateSpace and get your book published without paying any setup fees or incurring any other costs except for the cost of ordering the proof copy of your just-printed book. (Even this cost is optional. You can proof-read your book online at no cost.)

Obviously, you should read and follow CreateSpace's "Submission Requirements" before formatting and uploading your PDF files. To find these requirements, go to **createspace.com** and type **submission requirements** in the search box to the right of the top menu bar. On the page that comes up, click **Book Interior Guidelines** or **Book Cover Guidelines**. You will find that the formatting procedures in my book will produce files that exactly match CreateSpace's submission requirements.

This "no-cost" option includes only minimal help from CreateSpace's staff of publishing professionals. You will have to navigate your own way through the publication process, although you can always use the "Contact Us" link to get your questions answered by e-mail.

To learn more about the "no-cost" option, click **Start a title for free** toward the top of CreateSpace's home page. (You will have to establish an account with CreateSpace in order to access this information.)

CreateSpace's Modest-Cost, Supported PDF Option

This "modest cost" option includes a variety of CreateSpace's publication services, each "package" of services having its own group of helps at ascending costs. The least expensive of these packages is labeled "Author's Express." At the time of this writing (November, 2013), this service costs $248. The

Author's Express package is well-worth the money, especially if you are self-publishing your first book. It includes the following benefits as stated by CreateSpace:

Help with making your files meet our submission requirements.

Assistance to complete adjustments within your files.

Direct contact with a Project Team who will work closely with you throughout the publishing process.

Phone support to answer your questions.

To find the Author's Express service, click **Explore paid services** toward the middle, right side of CreateSpace's home page. On the page that comes up, click **Author's Express** under "Standard Value Solutions." An "Author's Express" page will then come up with a **Contact Us** link for those who want to buy this service. However, you won't have to follow this link if you contact Whitney Strachan directly. She will take care of logging your purchase and of directing you to options for making payment.

CreateSpace's Discontinued Pro Plan
CreateSpace has discontinued its "Pro Plan," but not the benefits of that plan. The benefits that authors formerly had to pay $39 per book to receive are now free of charge. For each book published, CreateSpace gives you increased royalties, it greatly reduces the cost of all books you order directly from

CreateSpace, and it also qualifies all of your books for CreateSpace's EDC or "Expanded Distribution Channel."

The EDC gives you three more distribution outlets in which to sell your books. CreateSpace lists them as:

CreateSpace Direct: make your book available directly to certified resellers through our wholesale website.

Bookstores and Online Retailers: make your book available to major online and offline retailers.

Libraries and Academic Institutions: make your book available to libraries and academic institutions throughout the U.S.

Submissions Required Before Uploading Your Files

Most self-publishing firms will require you to submit various items of information about yourself and your book before and sometimes after they provide you with a link for uploading your PDF files. For CreateSpace, this information includes the following items:

Title of Your Book
Subtitle (if applicable)
Description (1,000 characters maximum, including spaces)*
Volume Number (if applicable)
ISBN
Imprint Name (Only if you provide the ISBN)
BISAC Category
Reading Level
This book previously published on
Country of Publication

Publication Date
Language
Search Keywords
Contributors
Authored By
Author's Biography (2.500 characters maximum)**
Trim Size
Interior Paper Color ("White" or "Cream")

*Description: Do your best work here, because what you write will appear on your book's detail page on Amazon.com. I suggest that you compose your description, as well as your bio, before accessing CreateSpace to enter your book's data.

**Author's Biography: The only advice I have to give you here is that you should try to include information that provides you with credentials for writing about your book's subject. Sure, you can end your bio with your wife's name, how many children you have, and where you live, but don't use this valuable space totally for human interest details.

Depending on your choice of the "no-cost" option or one of the "modest cost" options, you may be asked to submit some of this data *before* uploading your files and some of it *after* uploading them. I have included it all in one list so that you will know what information to prepare in advance.

Uploading Your PDF Files
Here, I'll explain only the basic steps for uploading your PDF files. Once you have entered all the preliminary information CreateSpace requires, on your Member Dashboard page you

will see "Attention Required" or "In Process" to the right of your book's title. Click on your book's **title.**

On the page that comes up, a window will appear for you to select the PDF "Interior file" you want to upload. Click the **Browse** button and navigate to the location on your computer where your PDF book block file is saved. Select that file and click **Open**. Its address will appear back in the Browse window on the previous page.

On that page, click **Save** at the bottom of the screen and a small box will say in sequence "Uploading," "Working," and "Processing." Then a second small box will come up saying "Automated Print Check" and "This will take just a few minutes."

After the Print Check completes its test, you are given the choice of "Launch Interior Reviewer" (to proof-read your book block online) or "Skip Interior Review." If the Print Check finds anything wrong, the errors it finds will be pointed out on the Interior Review. Then you will have to correct them on your original Word document, convert it to PDF, and go through the submission process again. If all is OK after Print Check, click **Save** at the bottom of the page.

Now use the same procedure to **Save** your book's PDF cover file. Follow the instructions until you can see and click **Submit files for review** at the bottom of the page. Your files are uploaded. Ah, what a thrill the first time you do this! (This procedure may change, but you can figure out how to do it.)

Once your uploaded files have been "Approved," CreateSpace will offer you the options of viewing a digital proof again, or ordering a printed proof, or doing both. Then you can either **Approve** your files or elect to **Change** your files.

If you click the **Change** button, you will have to modify your original Word document, re-convert it to PDF, and re-upload it to CreateSpace.

If you click the **Approve** button, your book will appear for sale on Amazon.com shortly thereafter.

Completing Your Royalty Profile

The first time you self-publish a book with any firm, you will be asked to supply information specifying the address or bank to which you want your royalties mailed or deposited. CreateSpace provides instructions for doing this.

After your book has moved into the final file creation phase of the book-making process, you will get an e-mail advising you to complete your royalty profile. Here are CreateSpace's instructions for doing this:

1. Log into your account.
2. In the "My Account" box of links on the left side of your screen, click **Edit Account Settings** at the bottom of the box.
3. Under "Royalty Payment Information," click **Manage the information and method in which you receive royalty payments**.

    a. <u>If you would like to be paid by direct deposit:</u> Complete all fields on the Royalty Payment Information page; be sure to select the **Request Direct Deposit** checkbox and enter your banking details.
    b. <u>If you prefer to be paid by paper check:</u> Complete only fields with asterisks, including **Payee Information**, **Tax Information**, and **Business Type**.

4. Click **Save**.

If you choose to be paid by a check in the mail, there is an $8 handling fee for each check payment. Surely you won't want to give back $8 dollars of your royalties each month. Why not choose the bank deposit option and keep this $8?

After finishing this, you'll be all set to receive the monetary fruits of your passionate labors.

From the time you first submit your book's title to CreateSpace, monitor your book's progress through the publication process by checking your Member Dashboard every day.

Chapter Twelve

NURTURING YOUR BOOK ON AMAZON.COM

I have included this final, brief chapter simply to advise you that just having your book listed for sale on Amazon.com will not automatically cause it to become a bestseller—unless, of course, you are already famous or infamous. In fact, if you do nothing to promote your book, you will see few, if any, sales except those copies you, yourself, order from Amazon or your publisher.

To help you understand just what you need to do to promote your book, I strongly suggest that you buy from Amazon *Sell Your Book on Amazon: Top-Secret Tips Guaranteed to Increase Sales for Print-On-Demand and Self-Publishing Writers* by Brent Sampson.

For other marketing advice, get *Aiming At Amazon: The NEW Business of Self Publishing or A How to Publish Your Books with Print on Demand and Online Book Marketing on Amazon.com* by Aaron Shepard. Also valuable is Steve Weber's book, *Plug Your Book: Online Book Marketing for Authors.* (See my bibliography at the back of this book.)

In fact, if you can afford them, almost all of the books in my bibliography offer you advice on how to nurture and promote your book's sales. But, if you can afford only one book on sales, buy Brent Sampson's.

CreateSpace allows you to follow the progress of your books' sales and the royalties they have earned. To find this information, log-in to your **Member Dashboard** site. Under "My Projects," you will find the titles of your books. At the bottom, right corner of the page, click **View Detailed Royalty Report**. On the "Reports" page that comes up, you will find a complete list of all your books' sales for the current month, along with their royalties that have been credited to your account.

Notice that the "Reports" page comes up on the "Royalty By Title" tab. For a more detailed report, click on the **Royalty Details** tab. Then on the page that comes up, click **Run Report** toward the bottom, right of the page. The "Results" page comes up, showing dates your books were sold, along with the royalties you made and other information.

To make these pages more easily accessible, I suggest that you add your "Member Dashboard" page and the "Results" page to your "Favorites Bar" or "Bookmarks Toolbar" at the top of your screen.

AUTHOR'S NOTE

An author is seldom without debt to other authors who have published books within his own genre. This book is built partly upon the knowledge I have gained from reading the books listed in my bibliography and partly upon the many, many explorations and experiments I have conducted on the possible uses of Microsoft Word and Adobe Acrobat.

Through trial and error, I have expanded much of the sometimes-general information I learned in these cited books to encompass exact, step-by-step procedures required for a complete, do-it-yourself, self-publishing strategy. In this book, I have designed these procedures specifically around the use of Word 2010.

Even so, my precise instructions for using Word 2010 may be useable with earlier versions of Word if you will *adapt* them to achieve their intended results.

And speaking of intended results, I have gone through this entire book and put to the test every instruction I have given you. Making as though I were an uninformed reader, I confirmed that anyone following these instructions would produce from their use ready-to-print, PDF files acceptable to virtually any self-publishing firm using a POD press.

I wish you many sales and abundant royalties.

Appendix

A CHART FOR BOOK COVER DESIGN, 6" x 9"

All commands and selections that must be clicked and all data that must be entered or selected are depicted in **bold** letters and numbers; all other defaults are left as they are. Titles of all dialog boxes are in UPPER CASE type.

To use this chart, just enter your own data in the underlined spaces and select options indicated. You must know your book's number of pages and spine width.

Book Specifications:
Trim Size: __6" x 9"__, No. Pages: __176__, Spine Width: __0.4"__
1. **Open** new Word document.

2. **Page Layout** tab/Page Setup group:
   Click **arrow** at bottom of Page Setup group
      PAGE SETUP dialog box:
         Paper tab
            Paper size:
               Width: __18"__, Height: __12"__

         Margins tab
            Orientation: **Landscape**
            Margins:
               Top: **1.5"**, Bottom: **1.5"**
               Left: **2.8"**, Right: **2.8"** (For 0.4" spine. Enter your
                         own figures for Left & Right margins.)
            OK/Ignore margins

3. **View** tab/Zoom group:
    Zoom/ZOOM dialog box:
      Zoom to
        Percent__**50%**__   **OK**

    Or: Use Zoom slider, lower, right of screen

4. **Page Layout** tab/Page Setup group:
    Columns
    Dropdown menu:
      More Columns/COLUMNS dialog box:
        Number of Columns __**2**__
          Width and Spacing
            Col #   Width: Spacing:
            1:   __**6"**__   __**0.4"**__   **OK**

5. **Page Layout** tab/Paragraph group:
    Indent
      Indent Left: **0.5**
      Indent Right: **0.5**

6. **Home** tab/Paragraph group:
    Apply **Show/Hide** indicator, position cursor top, left in left column, press & hold down **Enter** on keyboard to fill both columns with **Show/Hide** symbol, return cursor to bottom in left column.

7. **Page Layout** tab/Page Setup group:
    Breaks
      PAGE BREAKS dialog box:
        Column

8. **Insert** tab/Text group:
    Text Box/BUILT-IN dialog box:
      Draw Text Box
        + : **Position** top, center left column, **click mouse**.

9. Drawing Tools & Format tabs/Size group:
   Shape Height: __9"__
   Shape Width**:**   __0.4"__ (Enter your book's spine width.)
                Press **Enter** on keyboard.

10. Drawing Tools & Format tabs/Arrange group:
    Icon that reads **Align Objects**, click **Align Center**
    Icon that reads **Align Objects**, click **Align Middle**

11. Drawing Tools & **Format** tabs/Text group:
    Text Direction **icon**, click **Rotate all text 90°**

12. Use Zoom slider (lower, right of screen) to enlarge text box to 150% or more.

13. Drawing Tools & Format tabs/Shape Styles group
    Arrow at bottom, right of box
       FORMATE SHAPE dialog box
         Layout & Properties **icon**
          Text Box
           0.05 in Left & Right windows, **Close**

14. **Home** tab/Click inside spine box
    Insert spine text: press **spacebar** for position desired,
    Font tab, select **font, font size, font color** (if wanted).
    Enter **title**, **author name**.

15. To center spine text (Click **cursor** inside spine's text box)
    Drawing Tools & **Format** tabs/Shapes & Styles group
       Arrow at bottom, right corner of box
         FORMAT SHAPES dialog box
          Layout & Properties **icon**
           Text Box/Internal Margins
            Click **down arrow** in box to right of "Right
            Margin" until figure in it reads **0**".
           Enter **0.08** (more or less) into box

16. To remove border around spine: Click inside spine box. Drawing Tools & **Format** tabs/Shape Styles group:
    Click **Shape Outline**.
    Click **No Outline**.

17. For colored cover, click *outside* the spine and then click the **Page Layout** tab on top menu bar. In "Page Background" group, click **Page Color**. From menu, **select** and **click** color desired. To color spine, click in spine and click **Format** under the "Drawing Tools" tab. In the "Shape Styles" group, click **Shape Fill**. Click cover's color. Or, select different spine color.

18. Right column: Center the cursor, select **font**, **font size**, **font color** (if any). Enter **title, sub-title** (if wanted) and **author name** at desired positions.

19. Insert desired **graphics** or **photos** in right column.

20. Left column: Enter **back cover blurb**. For colored cover when using self-publishing firm other than CreateSpace, insert **text box** and **bar code**. Insert **photo** (if wanted).

21. **Save**.

BIBLIOGRAPHY

These books are listed in the order that I believe each to be of most value to you as supplements to this book. By following my instructions, you won't actually need to buy any of them, but do try to obtain at least a few, anyway. All of them are for sale on Amazon.com.

The prices listed here are those quoted by Amazon at the time of this writing. Prices may change. Several of these books cost much more when bought in retail book stores.

Shepard, Aaron. *Perfect Pages: Self Publishing with Microsoft Word, or How to Design Your Own Book for Desktop Publishing and Print on Demand (Word 97-2003 for Windows, Word 2004 for Mac)*. Olympia, Washington: Shepard Publications, 2006. 158 pages. $10.00.

Sampson, Brent. *Sell Your Book on Amazon: The Book Marketing COACH Reveals Top-Secret "How-to" Tips Guaranteed to Increase Sales for Print-on-Demand and Self-Publishing Writers*. Denver, Colorado: Outskirts Press, Inc., 2007. 184 pages. $14.95.

Poynter, Dan. *Dan Poynter's Self-Publishing Manual: How to Write, Print and Sell Your Own Book*. Santa Barbara, California: Para Publishing, 15th edition, 2006. 472 pages. $13.57. ($19.95 in bookstores, 16th edition now out)

Rosenthal, Morris. *Print-on-Demand Book Publishing: A New Approach to Printing and Marketing Books for Publishers and Authors.* Springfield, MA: Foner Books, 2004. 176 pages. $13.19.

Shepard, Aaron. *Aiming at Amazon: The NEW Business of Self Publishing, or How to Publish Your Books with Print on Demand and Online Book Marketing on Amazon.com.* Olympia, Washington: Shepard Publications, 2007. 208 pages. $10.20. (Please see Aaron's note on "changes at Amazon," posted on his book's detail page on Amazon.)

Ross, Tom & Marilyn. *The Complete Guide to Self Publishing.* Cincinnati, Ohio: Writer's Digest Books, 4th edition, 2002. 521 pages. $20.98.

Padova, Ted. *Adobe Acrobat X PDF Bible.* Indianapolis, Indiana: Wiley Publishing, Inc., 2011. 936 pages. $29.69. (Earlier edition $44.99 in bookstores)

The University of Chicago Press. *The Chicago Manual of Style.* Chicago and London: 16th edition, 2010. 1026 pages. $39.67. (Earlier edition $55.00 in bookstores)

Weber, Steve. *Plug Your Book! Online Book Marketing for Authors, Book Publicity through Social Networking.* Falls Church, VA: Weber Books, 2007. 204 pages. $12.76.

ABOUT THE AUTHOR

After spending 23 years working in the electronics industry (16 years with Texas Instruments), Edwin Scroggins decided to change careers. To prepare himself to enter the field of Christian Education, Edwin earned a Bachelor's degree in Biblical Education and a Master's degree in Adult and Continuing Education, both obtained while working full time to support his family.

In 1978, Edwin joined the Dallas Bible College as a member of its faculty. He served there as Assistant to the President (writing proposals to gain grants from various foundations), as a classroom teacher (of writing and church publicity), and as an administrator and developer of Bible courses and study guides for the college's External Studies Department.

Edwin's literary publications include *Prophecy for Today*, published by Dallas Bible College in 1971, and *Bible Prophecy in a Nutshell*, published by BookSurge in 2007. His two-volume memoir, *Strawberry Lane* and *Return to Strawberry Lane*, were both published by BookSurge in 2007. *How I Built My Retreat Cabin in the Woods and Lived to Write About It* was published by BookSurge in 2008. In 2010, CreateSpace published Edwin's *The Promise and Passion of Christ the King*.

Since 1961, Edwin has lived in Richardson, Texas with Alma, his beloved wife of 61 years. Following her death in

April, 2011, he collected some of her memoirs, journal entries, prayers, and artwork and compiled them in a book entitled *Songs in the Night: Memories of Alma Grace Scroggins* (published by CreateSpace in 2012).

Edwin continues to live in the house he and Alma owned for over 50 years.

HOW TO ORDER

To order this book and others by Edwin Scroggins, go to www.amazon.com, select "Books" from the Amazon category menu, and then enter the author's name in the search box. On the page that comes up, click on the book's title to access details and ordering information. (You must submit a valid credit card number to order.)

If you found *How to Self-Publish Your Book Using Microsoft Word 2013* valuable, please post a review for it on Amazon.com.

NOTES

Made in the USA
San Bernardino, CA
03 May 2014